GABRIEL MARCEL

Gabriel Marcel

An Introduction

by

Thomas J. M. van Ewijk

Translated by

Matthew J. van Velzen

DEUS BOOKS
PAULIST PRESS
(Paulist Fathers)
Glen Rock, N. J.

A Deus Books Edition of the Paulist Press, 1965,
by special arrangement with Lannoo Publishers,
Tielt and The Hague.

NIHIL OBSTAT: Robert E. Hunt, S.T.D.
                               Censor Librorum

IMPRIMATUR: ✠ Thomas A. Boland, S.T.D.
                               Archbishop of Newark

June 2, 1965

COVER DESIGN: Claude Ponsot

Library of Congress   *142.092*
Catalog Card Number: 65-24043

Published by the Paulist Press
Editorial Office: 304 W. 58th St., N.Y., N.Y. 10019
Business Office: Glen Rock, New Jersey 07452

Manufactured in the
United States of America
24

About the Author

Thomas J. M. van Ewijk: Born in Amsterdam, 1934, he is working in the world of books. At first he published poems and short stories in various magazines. His declamatorium *De Leerling en de Engel* (The Disciple and the Angel) had performances in two Amsterdam churches. His published works are *Weesgegroet* (Ave Maria; poems); *Het Oor van Malchus* (Malchus' Ear—novel; *Midden onder U* (In the Midst of You—novelette); *Wilde Zwijnen, Tamme Varkens* (Wild Swine, Tame Pigs—two novelettes). His philosophical interest is especially directed at contemporary philosophy of which he has made an extensive study.

TO
MARIA-HELENA, MY MOTHER

"Nothing in the world is as difficult to patent as philosophy; nothing is as hard to make exclusively one's own."

Gabriel Marcel—*Du refus à l'invocation*

"Philosophy means: to be en route. Its questions are more important than its answers, and every answer leads to a new question."

Karl Jaspers—*Inleiding tot de Philosophie*

Contents

Contents

Preface

THE purpose of this introductory work is to acquaint the reader with the French philosopher and dramatist Gabriel Marcel. But it is concerned only with Marcel the philosopher.

In talking about philosophy with friends, acquaintances and colleagues, who mostly belong to the educated laity, we find that most often discussion comes to a dead end with some concluding statement like "It's just so much useless talk", or "Yes, philosophers know how to present complicated ideas on paper, but these ideas no longer have anything to do with reality."

For most people, philosophy is a different and distant world where philosophers continually write, reason and argue in a mysterious jargon that is of no use to society. "Philosophy doesn't improve us, it makes us worse. Nietzsche and Sartre prove that", people say.

But we can take comfort in Karl Jaspers' idea that one cannot escape philosophy: he who dismisses it is unconsciously a philosopher himself. We gladly agree with him, for this attitude of dismissal, remarkably enough, is not generally due to intellectual laziness—on the contrary, people do think and discuss passionately—but to some kind of peevishness, or even resentment of all this pompous and mysterious learning.

Still, this learning exercises an unmistakable and profound influence on man's thinking. But philosophy does not seem to fare differently from poetry: it is destined for the few. And those few can still be divided into two groups: philosophers and professional philosophers. This distinction is indeed meant ironically, but all the same it is based on an inescapable fact: poets are only read by poets, philosophers only by philosophers.

However, we want to point out that the number of interested people—among whom we count ourselves—is on the increase, and so is the love for wisdom, or rather, for reflection.

In his booklet *Wat is Existentialisme?* (chapter 1: "Gabriel Marcel") Dr. Bernard Delfgaauw writes that one could raise the question of whether thinking about philosophical problems serves any useful purpose if these problems are, after all, essentially insoluble mysteries. Such an objection is typical in this technological age, but the fact that a problem is insoluble does not imply that it would be unfruitful to reflect on it:

"Reflection on a philosophical problem puts myself and the world in a light that would otherwise escape me. Through philosophical reflection I understand why I am in this world and how I must be in the world. And although this understanding is only a partial one, the thinking man finds here a guide that science cannot give him. The positive sciences must turn away such questions. They can only be put meaningfully in religion and philosophy." Moreover, we must not forget: "Philosophy is and remains, as Plato was the first to say, wonderment."

It is one of the great merits of Gabriel Marcel that his philosophy and his way of philosophizing is not only accessible to the professional philosopher, but also to anyone who wants to reflect on the meaning of his own personal existence. Popularly speaking, philosophy for Marcel means "going out in the street", entering into conversation with people. That is why he calls his way of thinking a form of neo-Socratism.

But this definitely does not mean that we have at last found a philosopher who satisfies our need for the help of a professional philosopher; on the contrary, every seriously minded person accepts some guidance when he tries to think philosophically. Philosophy is not some experimental twaddle! We hope that after meeting Gabriel Marcel the reader will get into discussion with him; that is, that he will study Marcel's work more thoroughly. Then our purpose in this introduction will have been fulfilled.

THOMAS J. M. VAN EWIJK

*AUTHOR'S NOTE: We have made use of the Dutch translations of Marcel's books *Etre et avoir, Homo Viator, L'homme problématique* and *Les hommes contre l'humain*. Therefore we have kept to the pagination of the Dutch translations of those works. To avoid confusion we want to point out that in our quotations, when we only give the page number, it refers to the last-named book in the preceding text.

1

Philosophy
and Christian Thinking

In Blaise Pascal's *Pensées* one finds the following
complaint:

"It is in vain, O man, that you are looking in yourself for the remedy for your miseries. All the light
that has been given to you will never bring you any
further than to the recognition that you will never
find either the truth or your salvation in yourself. The
philosophers had promised you this, and they have
not been able to make their promise good. They do
not know what really is your salvation, nor what your
real condition is. How could they have found remedies for your ills, when they do not even know them?"

May we suppose that these words are outmoded
today? Are present-day philosophers aware of our
ills and have they found the remedies? We are almost

13

inclined to answer in the affirmative. Because it seems to us that there has never been a time like ours in which many philosophers—believers or unbelievers—have begun an intensive search for the remedies for our ills, and with such great awareness of those ills. Philosophy has become more sympathetic (we are thinking of the Greek *sympatheo tini*: to feel with somebody); it is closer to us, it is in conversation *with* us.

"He who notices the trend in my philosophical work must see it in its entirety as a persistent, unceasing fight against the spirit of abstraction", Gabriel Marcel writes in the Preface of his book *Les hommes contre l'humain*. It is that spirit of abstraction against which Pascal is really protesting in his complaint about the philosophers of his time. Still, it would be unjust merely to ignore this spirit, all the more so since for centuries it has dominated philosophy, until—and here we speak in the mind of A. N. Whitehead who in his book *Science in the Modern World* breaks a lance for abstraction—philosophy and science, which had been going hand in hand, parted and began each to seek its own path.

How far is this a gain or a loss? It is not up to us to decide. Pascal, a genius in both mathematics and the sciences, is to the informed Christian also a great Christian thinker and psychologist. He understood the ills and knew the remedies, which cannot so easily be reduced to abstractions because we are too intimately involved in them. Here we touch upon such experiences as faith, hope and love, with which the philosophers of Pascal's time apparently did not concern themselves.

If the stature of a man like Pascal might justify a plea for an alliance between philosophy and science, he himself rises above both of them as a religious thinker. A phrase like "to ridicule philosophy, is really to philosophize" (*Pensées*) comes from the pen of a man who thoroughly knew the game of the spirit of abstraction, but whose thinking has gone into the direction of "being", where God is not merely a part of a philosophical system but the subject of each and every chapter.

In the preceding lines we wanted to make a distinction between philosophy in general and Christian thinking. When man can be seen continually between the lines—with his belief and disbelief, with his hope and despair, his love and lovelessness—and makes his heartbeat heard, there is no longer room for a system; it becomes necessary to break with tradition. Philosophizing then becomes something so personal that it acquires the range of an important and unforgettable "meeting" and loses some of its limitation.

In the opinion of Nicholas Berdyaev, "It is precisely by breaking the relation between Christianity and certain definite forms of philosophy that philosophy gains in freedom" (*Das Ich und die Welt der Objekte*—The "I" and the Objective World). This interesting and original thinker sketches for us the positions of the believing and the unbelieving philosopher. The unbelieving philosopher is a man of defective experience and restricted vision. There are entire worlds that he does not know exist. Berdyaev credits the unbelieving philosopher with only a poor understanding because he considers his own limitations as the limit of "being". His tragedy is that he does not know what tragedy is: "His freedom is his bondage."

To have an open mind for other worlds, for the meaning of "being", is the proper quality of "believing". The believing philosopher also wants to be free

with regard to his philosophical insight, but not in-
frequently this brings him into conflict with the common way of thinking about his faith. Berdyaev cites as
an example, among other things, the authority of
theology, which suspects the believing philosopher or
even accuses him of heresy! Here is a question of
conflict between belief in relation to God and belief
in relation to a religious denomination.

Berdyaev continues (and we quote him literally):

"The greatest tragedy, however, is in another
sphere. The philosopher experiences this tragedy, as
every great tragedy, not so much when he confronts
others as when he confronts himself. In his free
understanding, which does not admit of any outside
restriction or ban, the philosopher cannot forget his
faith and that which reveals itself to him in it. We are
not concerned here with the external problems of the
relation of his philosophy to the others, the represen-
tatives of religion, but with the internal problem of
the relation of his philosophical insight to his own
belief, to his own personal experience, which opens
up other worlds to him" (*Das Ich und die Welt der
Objekte*).

Other worlds . . . This has a mysterious sound, this
puts the word "mystery" on our lips. This is what
the adventure of the believing philosopher encounters. He may perhaps lose his way, the road that he
follows may be a dead end, but he may also lose himself in the mystery. In that case he enters upon the
ground that can be reached by contemplation, or
adoration, as Marcel would say, then philosophy
stops being philosophy. The word "contemplation",
however, should not deter us. In history there have
been more men among the simple of heart than among
the philosophers who have reached this territory.

Christian thinking—and here we mean Christian without any bitter connotation or special sense of learnedness—can enable us to think along with the philosopher. His adventure becomes ours. Martin Heidegger has coined an unforgettable word when he says in his main work *Sein und Zeit*: *"Das Denken soll denkender werden"* ("Thinking should become more-thinking"). It is, in our opinion, precisely the preeminently Christian thinker Gabriel Marcel who has succeeded, in spite of the capricious and unsystematic character of his philosophy, in making our thinking "more-thinking". Perhaps he also makes us more believing. His philosophy is different.

In his Introduction to Marcel's book (in the Dutch translation) *L'homme problématique,* Dr. B. Delfgaauw writes:

"Here we see no search for an impersonal system, but a system of thinking from one's own personal being. The author of this book is not in the first place someone who contemplates the world, but one who has been struck by the world, the world here having the double meaning of internal and external world, of microcosm and macrocosm. Thinking is for the author not just an optional game, but a necessity in order that he may clarify existence."

Before we become involved solely with Gabriel Marcel as a philosopher and with the principal ideas of his philosophy, we want to stress that we are not presenting a philosophy that we consider as the only true one. Just like every philosophy, it is another attempt to find the truth. Here Montaigne's saying applies: "For we have been created to seek the truth; to possess it has been reserved to a higher power" (*Essais*, iii, 8).

This seems to us a humble standpoint to start from.

2

A Man,
a Philosopher

GABRIEL MARCEL was born in Paris on December
7, 1889. He spent the greater part of his youth
in Sweden. He also stayed often in Germany, England
and Italy. His father held important posts as Privy
Councillor and French Ambassador at Stockholm and
was later appointed Director of the Beaux-Arts, the
Bibliothèque Nationale and the Musées Nationaux.
Thanks to his highly educated father, the son profited
very much from the many trips they made together,
during which they visited numerous cities of cultural
interest. At an early age the young Marcel came into
contact with well-known personalities in the political
and literary worlds. An avid and penetrating reader,
he did not confine his interest to French writers only
but also directed his attention especially to authors
from other countries than his native France.

His works, of course, reflect that he was widely
read, and for this reason alone they make a favorable

impression; they show no trace of the suffocating
chauvinism that is typical of most Frenchmen. On the
contrary, Marcel's work is open-minded; he engages
us in a dialogue, not as a Frenchman but as a man,
as a neighbor. And whenever the native philosophical
vocabulary falls short, he resorts to the German or
English language.

The agnostic atmosphere in which he grew up, however, was not a happy one for this extremely sensitive
and very intellectual boy. Moreover, he was an only
child and at the age of four lost his mother. The
sudden death of Madame Marcel had a profound influence on his childhood and was continually on his
mind. Later in life, he would admit that she had
always been "with him". They rarely spoke about
her in the family circle, and a respectful fear kept him
from asking the questions that made her "disappear-
ance" such an awe-inspiring but tormenting mystery
for him. But his aunt (whom his father later married) felt quite certain that Gabriel had no problems
that she herself could not completely solve.

His mother's death marks the beginning of Marcel's thinking about God and the hereafter. What
happens to us after we die? This question affects all
of us, believers or unbelievers. It is literally a question of life and death. And what is philosophy but a
question of life and death?

Gabriel Marcel's aunt, who became the young boy's
stepmother, led him into a dreary and gloomy No-
Man's-Land, where she left him standing alone in a
cold and drizzly rain of despair and stern admoni-
tions. She had the very best of intentions, as did his
father, who also failed him in that his position should
have enabled him to give Gabriel more than just the
required esthetic formation.

An already physically weak and hypersensitive child cannot help feeling spiritually oppressed in such an atmosphere. He suffered from high blood pressure, which often reached an alarming degree.

The bad impression that this description of Gabriel's childhood may have made on some readers should be corrected to some extent. Young Gabriel loved his father and his stepmother very much, and these people in turn surrounded him with their most tender care and with all the affection they were capable of. The possibility that he would become a spoiled little boy did not seem unlikely, the more so since from his earliest years he had never had any friends of his own age. And there was nothing that he needed more than friendship. Ever since his early childhood he took a lively and spontaneous interest in "the other one", for whom he felt interest and sympathy.

"Nothing is lost for a man—I am convinced of this and I firmly believe it—if he experiences a great love or a true friendship, but everything is lost for the one who is alone", he confided to Roger Troisfontaines (*De l'existence à l'être,* p. 18, vol. 1).

During World War I (1914-1918) Marcel, who was not physically fit for the rigors of military life, dedicated himself to the service of the Red Cross, tracing lost persons. Day in, day out he received parents, wives and lovers who had placed their last hope in him. In this way he was confronted with the indescribable suffering of those who stayed behind, and all too often he was forced to feel that he was only a powerless spectator at a tragedy, where tears were more eloquent than words.

During the winter of 1916-1917, he once let himself be induced by one of those unhappy ones who

wanted to have certainty at all cost, to take part in
spiritistic séances. At that time he did not know his
own mind. This expedient did not satisfy him, however, and he finally rejected it. But perhaps these experiences make it clear that Gabriel Marcel really is
the obvious philosopher (not the only one!) to develop such penetrating and edifying philosophical
ideas as those of the "personal meeting" and of hope.
On March 23, 1927, at the age of thirty-nine, he put
the seal on a conscious choice of faith. At first he
had felt more attracted to Protestantism, but he was
finally baptized and received into the Catholic Church.

The long and difficult road that led him to this
Church will not be described here, in retrospect, merely for the sake of completeness. We will not venture
to tell the story here, or even to sum up the facts in
a so-called "conversion story", which personally has
never been very convincing to this writer. A conversion is a far too intimate and overpowering adventure
for that. It is something for which Marcel may be
envied. His philosophy, which is also partly deter-
mined by his choice of faith, will reveal, among other
things, what the results have been of this choice.

We will conclude this biographical sketch by men-
tioning the special influence that music has exercised
on Marcel's life and thought. He is an accomplished
pianist himself. During his youth he used to play
improvisations on the piano for as long as three hours
a day; he would be completely engrossed in the inspiration of the moment and translate his thoughts
into sound. "Perhaps that was my real vocation", he
muses. "There especially I feel myself creating. Music
has guided my thinking in the right direction" (*De
l'existence à l'être,* p. 25, vol. 1). More than many a
book, it was music that could shape and broaden his

ideas. Bach's music especially appealed to him and
he says that Christian life really has come to him
through the Passions and the Cantatas.

In his book *Les hommes contre l'humain* there is
a chapter entitled *"Révaluation de l'honneur"* that begins like this:

"I had a remarkable experience recently. I was
coming home from a concert where I had heard Bach
played and I experienced in myself a revival of a feeling or rather of a certainty that seems to have been
lost in our time: the honor of being human."

We will come back to this later.

It should be pointed out here that apart from his
philosophical works Gabriel Marcel has also written
a great number of plays for the stage, and he is, moreover, working as a literary critic. However, we must
restrict ourselves to the philosopher and leave the
dramatist and the critic out of our consideration. But
for a better understanding of Marcel's work we should
not lose sight of the fact that he is as much a philosopher as a dramatist, "both with the same aim in view:
to try to penetrate the essence of man" (Dr. B.
Delfgaauw: *Wat is Existentialisme?*).

In his philosophical autobiography *My Road to
Self-Knowledge,* Nicholas Berdyaev, an exile from
Russia, here and there devotes some lines to Marcel,
which date from the 'twenties. A few of his interesting
remarks may well be appropriate in this connection:

"I must mention here also the philosophical gatherings at the home of Gabriel Marcel. They were, I
believe, the only philosophical gatherings in Paris that
have had any permanent results and were continued
for a long time. There used to be many people present
at those meetings which were held in a private home:

not only Frenchmen, but also foreigners, Germans, Russians, Spaniards. Many young people who were interested in philosophy came there as well. This was probably the only place in France where problems of phenomenology and existential philosophy were discussed. The names of Husserl, Scheler, Heidegger and Jaspers were frequently mentioned. Here there was no question of being imprisoned within French culture."

A little further on, Berdyaev writes about his host: "Marcel himself was considered as a philosopher of the existentialist type. He was more at home in German philosophy than the other Frenchmen."

It is indeed true that Marcel grew up in German Idealism (Kant, Hegel, Fichte). Later, he came under the strong influence of the great philosopher Bergson, who shows in his works that he is opposed to materialism and positivism. He recognized the possibility of metaphysical knowledge and believed in the existence of extrasensual reality.

Marcel broke with rationalism and lapsed more or less into traditionalism. After his transition to the Catholic faith, he looked to mysticism and to members of the Oxford Group for every expression and revelation of the Spirit who breathes where He will of God's activity in this world.

For the rest, he admitted of no curtailing of his intellectual freedom after his "conversion", and he wrote and spoke as freely as before. Marcel is no slavish follower; in virtue of his vocation he simply cannot permit himself to be one. In him is manifested the grace of that freedom which—we are discovering this more and more in our time—is also the right of Catholics. Marcel resolutely refuses to be labeled an "existentialist". He is perfectly right, in that through a psychological and phenomenological approach to human existence he wants to penetrate the extrasensual, the metaphysical reality of "being". First and foremost he aims at an ontology that is concerned with "being" as such. And, as Dr. H. Robbers, S.J. says, for Marcel to practice ontology means that the philosopher enters consciously into his own situation, in which he finds that he is bound up with "being" (*engagé*). Here, mystery and ontology coincide (*Bijdragen,* Neth., S.J. iv, 1941, p. 1-27—philosophical magazine published by Dutch Jesuits).

But what is the characteristic mark of an existentialist philosopher? One of his main sources for thought is literature. His philosophy maintains close contact with the spontaneous experiences of existence, which are expressed especially in plays, but also in novels and poetry. The existentialist philosopher makes those existential experiences part of his philosophical reflection and further elaborates them. Also the approach to the object, which is rationalistic philosophy must be reached only through thinking, is different. Existentialism does not put object against subject, it does not objectivize in the developing process of knowing; it attempts to approach the object through existential experiences such as fidelity and infidelity, hope and despair, courage and fear. These "experiences" must be probed and laid bare. Existentialism is loaded with sentiment. In both these respects Gabriel Marcel is an existentialist, although with the important difference that his philosophy is positively directed at "being" and does not produce a pessimistic atheism (Sartre) that mainly defends "non-being".

Marcel's method of philosophy is a "Christian existentialism", in which faith and hope play the princi-

pal parts. He himself calls his philosophy neo-Socratism. Just as Socrates in Athens would start a conversation in order to help a person discover some truth
already present in his own consciousness, Marcel,
likewise, tries by his work to come into discussion
with us and to throw a new clarifying light on our
existential experiences. He is present in his philosophy
as a person in whom we can recognize and understand
ourselves and the events that take place around us.

In his *Eloge de la philosophie* the existentialist
Maurice Merleau Ponty writes:

"In order to rediscover the real purpose of philosophy, we must remember that even the philosophical
writers whom we read, and who we are ourselves,
always recognized as their model a man who did not
write, who did not teach, at least not in the chairs of
learning of the State, but who addressed himself to
those he met in the streets, and who had difficulties
with public opinion and with the ruling power: I
mean Socrates" (p. 48).

Socrates, who could learn nothing from the fields
and the trees, but who learned from the people in the
city (Plato, *Phaedros*) sought out man enclosed in his
own limited personality in order to teach him to live
in the world, to know his fellowmen and God. This
is Marcel's aim, and he rightly summarizes his system
under the name neo-Socratism.

Somewhere above we have called his philosophy
capricious and unsystematic. In this connection we
may point to such names as Kierkegaard and
Nietzsche, who also cannot be called "systematic philosophers". Marcel's philosophical work should indeed be called one great flight of thought rather than
an easily surveyable system, neatly put together in

large and small compartments. It is an intricately woven pattern of ideas. Marcel regrets this. He knows that he will never be able to write the systematic treatise he had wanted to write: "I feel a certain annoyance with myself, when I find that I certainly have not kept to the rules of the philosophical game, which have been followed almost without exception until this day", he acknowledges in *Homo Viator* (p. 11).

But does not every system exactly imply abstraction? Is it not a fact that a concrete philosophy such as Gabriel Marcel's ultimately rejects the classical, rationalistic and idealistic philosophies precisely because they occupy themselves with abstractions and try to encompass reality in a system? A concrete philosopher is capricious and unsystematic for the reason that he continually maintains contact with reality, simply cannot exist without it, and reacts philosophically to the experiences of "being" that he personally feels and realizes.

Positive science has a merely objective knowledge of reality—at least that is what it claims—and excludes all subjectivity. Science only proceeds by way of abstraction and is not concerned with "being" and the subjective experiences of "being", which do not change anything in the object. The object alone is of importance, and nothing else; it is separated from its surroundings and dissected in all its component parts. It is quite clear that this "knowledge" does not admit of any mystery. Every man is in himself a mystery. Science manages to reduce him to a problematic, analyzable thing.

The existentialist method of knowing resolutely rejects such objectivity. A purely objective knowledge of things in themselves is impossible; knowledge must in a sense be permeated with subjectivity because our knowledge, after all, has its origin in perception, which is intimately connected with our existence. Positive knowledge, therefore, does not penetrate into "being" and it bypasses existence. Insofar as every positive science operates by abstraction, its object is stripped of its concrete existence and, therefore, also of its "being", namely, of its mystery. In this way it becomes the study-object for the scientist. It is basically this method of abstraction that Marcel criticizes.

Why does he think that this method of abstraction cannot be justified as a scientific procedure? We are inclined to think that it is mainly his heart that inspires Marcel's attitude of refusal in this respect. And surely not without reason. Marcel is not opposed to science, but he continually points to the danger that its students may neglect or even deny "being" to such an extent that not only their conclusions but their whole attitude may have disastrous consequences for society. Positive science has a right to its own methods of approach, but it happens all too frequently that it sets itself up as a way of life or a philosophy. And it is against this that Marcel protests.

We cannot escape asking ourselves the question whether existentialist philosophy more or less abandons reason—something that it ultimately cannot do without—because reason does not reach that strictly defined and exact clarity that is a condition *sine qua non* for scientific thinking. Where the object of thinking is loaded with feeling, one can hardly require that kind of clarity. Where the one system is bent on rejecting questions, the other one conjures them up by the dozen. Gabriel Marcel realizes this. "A concrete philosophy", he writes in *Du refus à l'invocation,* "is a philosophy of the thinking mind itself; it cannot maintain itself except by a kind of dangerous and continuous acrobatics. I know beforehand that in what will follow, expression and terminology will always leave something to be desired" (p. 21).

An unpredictable and dramatic thinker such as Marcel has no sympathy for a rational kind of logic; he always tries to express himself as concretely as possible; he is thinking from the standpoint of really existing situations and actions. He continually searches for the most striking ways of expression. Does he succeed in this? We have made the remark that existentialist philosophy, too, cannot dispense with reason. Well, where reason permits—and reason permits a lot with Marcel—he has certainly succeeded.

In having an eye for experiences that can clarify much about reality but still never obtain scientific clarity, Marcel achieves a personal method of dialectics. In the following chapters we will probe into this method and try to become somewhat familiar with it, to the extent possible in this brief introduction to one of the most important thinkers of our time.

3

"My" Body

SOMEONE has died. People have arranged a room in which he has been laid out. Relatives and friends come to see how he looks and to express their sympathy. One of them remarks that he looks as if he were asleep, to which the widow answers:

"Ah yes, when I see him lying there like that, at least I have the feeling that he is still here. But to-morrow they will come to take him away. And that is what I dread so much. Because then I will be sure that I have lost him."

The presence of the body of the deceased still holds some meager consolation for that woman. The concrete tie between his body and the world of which she is a part has not yet been completely severed for her, because he is still there; he looks as if he were asleep. The body is not merely lying there as an instrument that at one time served some person, but as "his" body

31

that helped to constitute his "personality". Death has destroyed this mysterious union and made the mystery of "man" bigger for those left behind. They will not be able to remember the deceased otherwise than in his corporality, or, to use Gabriel Marcel's expression, as *être incarné* (incarnate being), someone who is connected with a body.

"*Etre incarné* (to be incarnate) is to present oneself as body, as this specific body, without being able to identify oneself with it, but also without being able to distinguish oneself from it" (*Du refus à l'invocation*, p. 31). Without my corporality (being incarnate in a body) I do not live my existence in this world. I confirm my existence by also confirming the existence of the world around me. This is only possible by my corporality, by which I am present to myself. My body shares in my experiences of existence. I confirm the existence of things in the world through the direct or indirect contact that they have with my body. For although my body may in many cases be understood as object, that does not take away the fact that *I experience* my body. And this living *experience* is subjective.

Suppose that I would deny the existence of my body? Impossible! For that would mean the end of all existence, my own included. Such a point of departure lacks all sense of reality. That is why Idealism has not succeeded in its attempt to make pure consciousness, not bound by any body, confirm its own existence and that of the world. My existence, in which the whole world coexists, does not admit of any philosophically abstract approach. It is therefore certainly not Marcel's idea to talk philosophically about object and subject outside concrete "being"; what he is after is the existential value of my experiences of existence. Also the things with which I come into contact in one way or another through my work, my hobbies, my needs, do indeed have an objective existence, but at the same time that they exist for me, they coexist *with* me. And therefore they exist in themselves, although they do not possess a conscious personality or subjectivity. Their existence is justified for me through their relation with my corporality.

Marcel's thinking here is realistic. He makes no philosophical separation of subject and object, the "I" and my body; he is not analyzing. The point of departure for his metaphysical knowledge of man is therefore man's experience as *être incarné*. "The 'incarnation'—central datum of metaphysics", he argues in *Etre et avoir* (p. 12). A little earlier he writes that "my body is being thought of insofar as it is *a* body, while at the same time my thinking gets stuck in the fact that it is *my* body".

Why does Marcel in his work always speak of "my" body? Because he wants to guard against taking a dualistic attitude toward the body and the conscious "I". If—in accordance with Descartes' dualism—I put my body in opposition to myself, then I stand as subject in opposition to the body as object. I will then have disembodied my personality and depersonalized my body. In this way there is only a question of *a* body; therefore, an abstraction, a thing. The "I" is no more than an individual who might just as well be someone else. Man has become a problem instead of a mystery.

We said just now that Gabriel Marcel does not make a philosophical distinction between the body and the conscious "I". "There is no such problem as that of the relation between soul and body. I cannot place myself in opposition to my body and ask myself what kind of relation it has to myself. Then my body, which exists for my thinking, would cease to be mine" (*Journal métaphysique*, p. 25).

In the beginning of this chapter we spoke of the man on his deathbed, of a "mystical union" that had been destroyed by death. To what extent? That remains as yet an open question to which no man can give the answer. Gabriel Marcel attempts to determine the relation of my conscious "I" to my body. I ask myself how far I *am* my body and how far I *have* my body; my body, which forms the "borderland" between being and having, my body, which determines my place in this world and characterizes my attitude in it. Through my body I *am* such and I *have* the things with which I can maintain my existence in this world. "Being" and "having", therefore, form no unity, but neither are they standing apart from one another; they reveal themselves in a "mysterious union".

Let us now ask ourselves what it means to say "I have my body". "To have" must not be considered here as identical with "to possess". Suppose that I possess my body; then we will have to strip the "I" of its wrapping. How can I then visualize the "I" as the possessor? And what remains of that "mysterious union"? "To have" the body therefore is not meant "to possess it", but "to have (it) at one's disposal". So my body is at my disposal? No. By virtue of my body I can dispose of the things of this world; it is the basis of all possession.

"The first object, the typical object with which I identify myself and which still escapes me, is my body; and it looks as if we find ourselves here, as it were, in the most hidden, the deepest hiding-place of Having. The body is the prototype of Having" (*Etre et avoir*,

p. 153). That is exactly the reason why I cannot "dispose" of my body, unless, maybe, I commit suicide.

The question of suicide is of considerable interest to Marcel. Suicide, however, puts the body out of use; the power to dispose of things is thereby eliminated. Hence, suicide is not disposing of something in the primary sense of the word. If we recapitulate the foregoing points, we can say that my body is the concrete tie between my conscious "I" and the world.

Marcel then wonders: can I now assert that my body is my instrument? One would think so. At first sight, it seems that I do indeed dispose of my body. But what is a real instrument?

"It seems that every instrument is meant to serve as an extension (of my body) in order to develop and extend a faculty that is present in principle and possessed by him who uses the instrument; this is as true of a knife as of a magnifying glass" (*Du refus à l'invocation,* p. 29). Knife and magnifying glass are among the things that I can use by virtue of my body. If now I consider my body as an instrument to handle instruments, then I consider it also as a thing that I merely use. Then there is again the question of "a" body that I objectivize (Descartes). I am disintegrating myself by not recognizing myself as *être incarné.* Let us remember for a moment our example of a deceased man: his body, which is lying there, still holds some sort of consolation for the widow who is left behind. Because he is still there, i.e., in this case, "his" body, which codetermined his "I" (personality), is still lying there. For that woman—at least for her sentiment—he is still "her husband". She will not say "There lies so-and-so's instrument", but "There lies so-and-so." My experience protests against the concept of "being-instrument" as such; therefore I am conscious of "being" my body rather than of handling it as an instrument.

With this, we have come to the second half of Marcel's question: how far can I say that I "am" my body?

It may seem from what has been said so far that the expression "I am my body" is perhaps more correct than "I have my body". But be careful, Marcel warns. Does it mean that I declare myself identical with my body as an object, as a thing? If so, then I am holding a materialistic view, because with that I would affirm: "My body is me; only my body exists." Marcel calls such an affirmation absurd. It is precisely characteristic of the body that it cannot exist by itself. Would such a thing as a world of bodies be possible?

"But who gives the body unity? Who thinks of it as a world? And on the other hand, in such a merely objective world what would be left of the principle of intimacy ('my' body), around which *l'orbite existentielle* (the existential sphere of influence) used to stabilize itself?" (*Du refus à l'invocation,* p. 30).

"I am my body" does not mean that I am some sort of a machine who without more ado is capable of perception and action. Then it is better to say that "I *have* the faculty to perceive and act." Marcel comes to a negative formulation, because the expression "I am my body" cannot be positively confirmed or denied: "It makes no sense to say that I am a certain something, connected in whatever manner to that other something that is or would be my body" (*Du refus à l'invocation,* p. 30). This links up with what he wrote earlier in his *Journal métaphysique* (p. 253): "It is not true to say that I am not my body, that my body is external to a certain central reality which I am myself."

If I therefore declare myself identical with my body
as others see it, then I underrate myself in my being-
human. Because in that way I will end up by no longer
recognizing and respecting myself and the other man
as *être incarné*; I am overlooking the mystery that we
are. Can I declare myself identical with my body as
subject? Yes, I can. But only provided that I ask this
counter-question: how can my body as subject really
be objectivized? Here we encounter an impossibility. Therefore, there cannot really be any question
of a pure identity, unless in an abstract and analytical
sense. As *être incarné* I am rising above that.

Recapitulating, we can therefore conclude: I live
my life amidst the things of this world, with which I
come in contact through my corporality—the aspect
of my "being"—by using them and by assimilating
them. "Being" and "having" are united within me in
a mysterious way.

In connection with this union this chapter will conclude with a brief explanation of *l'épreuve* (the trial),
which will have to furnish the proof of our reality in
"being". Am I really in my own eyes and in those of
the other man the one whom I imagine myself to be?

The meaning and the value of my life will indeed
become clear through the trials which I undergo.
Every man is exposed to the trials of his corporality;
repeatedly he finds himself at the crossroads: in one
direction, the way to mere having (the unreal being);
in the other, the way to the real "being", which ultimately leads to transcendency. But: "It literally looks
as if my body is devouring me" (*Etre et avoir,* p. 159).

We need not argue the truth and the tragedy of this
statement. The viewpoint of the materialist, "My body
alone exists, I myself am nothing" (*Journal métaphysique*), is its exact parallel. The materialist has

equated his body with his inner self and regards it as a cherished possession.

The more intimately I cling to my body, the more I lose in being my inner self. Besides, the situation in which I find myself through my corporality is an historical situation, because, as Marcel says, "My corporality includes what we may call historicity. A body is a history, or more exactly: a body is that in which a history ends, and in which it is recorded" (*Etre et avoir,* p. 32). Moreover, by my corporality I am subject to time. And what is time? One continuous change; one event succeeds another. Especially today, when almost everything depends on "speed", time appears to be a dictatorial agitator whose main quality is inconstancy.

I try now to secure myself in order not to be dragged along with the current of events. But the unexpected and the unforeseen only too often prove stronger than my safety measures. The trial is now that the "I" completely wraps itself up in the situation of the moment and does not seek *engagement* (to commit itself to the future)! In this way the events of my life are in danger of becoming detached from one another. They can be compared to beads, which neatly laid out one next to the other give the impression of forming a necklace, but which on being touched roll away in all directions; they do not form a connected whole because I have overlooked the thread—the meaning of life.

To avoid this trial I can shirk my responsibility with regard to life. I can lock myself up in the so-called unchangeable world of abstraction and objectivity and entertain the illusion that I am standing above it. But I shall never be able to create an unchangeable world for myself; capricious reality will

see to that. And does it not point to a lack of personality, when I try to shirk my responsibility?

I can therefore wrap myself up in the situation of
the moment, or I can withdraw to an unchangeable
world, but there is still a third possibility open to me:
from the instability of time I can place situations within the stability of my "being"; I make them a part of
myself and thus fix them in the great whole of past,
present and future.

"I am dependent on my past, which in turn is also
dependent on me. The present will only then give a
decisive meaning to my past, which remains unde-
cided, when my past will have been linked up with
my life as a whole. The act by which I assimilate the
past is, therefore, to a great extent similar to the act
by which I face the present. They both fix me im-
movably in a situation so that I am available for the
future" (Pierre Colin—*Existentialisme chrétien,* p.
56).

Thus my personality is able to resist time, which is
repeatedly in danger of losing its continuity, and to
overcome it and to dominate history: "Fill the earth
and subdue it; rule over the fishes of the sea, and the
fowls of the air, and over all living creatures that move
upon the earth" (Genesis 1, 28). It is only by linking
myself up with the future that I have really put myself
at the disposal of the divine plan of salvation.

My span of life literally runs into a dead end. In
this respect time is for me a trial. Especially when I
remember that in an objective and technological
world, death is a meaningless and physical affair.

But why then the fear of death?

If I experience death existentially as the end of my
life and the negation of my "being", as the "ultimate

problem of nothingness", then my trial will be in-
creased to the point of despair. Here lies for Gabriel
Marcel the seed of metaphysics—*l'exorcisation du
désespoir* (the exorcism of despair) to which we will
come back later.

4

Sources of "Being"

First and Second Reflection

Before we take more accurate bearings on those experiences that bring us into contact with "being", we must first point out that Gabriel Marcel distinguishes between a first and a second reflection.

The first reflection restricts itself to objective knowledge. From the preceding chapters the reader may already have understood clearly that this objective knowledge implies that the thing is placed as object before the thinking subject. And not only the thing, I myself as thinking subject can also become object for thought; I, too, can be analyzed both spiritually and physically and be defined and characterized as to my whole content. It is no longer a matter of "my" existence or "my" body, it is a matter of "an" existence of "a" body. In this way both experience and abstraction are the methods of knowing, by which we find ourselves in the field of science, which also reduces man, his body and his "I" to a thing.

"Perhaps it is possible to prove that the 'I' must assume the appearance of an empirical 'I', but then there is in fact only a question of the emiprical 'I' *in general*. However, the empirical 'I' in general is a fiction. What exists and what counts is the individual, the real individual that I am, with all the incredible ramifications of his experience, with all those details of the concrete adventure that he must live, he and no other" (*Homo Viator*, p. 119).

The second reflection, also sometimes called *recueillement,* attempts to go beyond the first in a dialectical way. It is here a question of reclaiming inundated territories: the existence and the subjectivity of reality. Thus the second reflection approaches "being". The aim of this process of thinking is, to participate again in things, to touch them in their "being", by which they exist with me and are connected with me.

As against mere "thinking", Gabriel Marcel distinguishes "thinking about", which supposes something or somebody about which or about whom I am thinking.

"Being" is really not *known,* but *recognized,* and this takes place through intuition. I have this intuition, although I do not immediately know that I have it; I realize it, namely, in experiences such as fidelity, faith and hope.

Metaphysics is for Marcel a reflection raised to a square: our faculty of thinking tries to attain it in the second reflection, in the *recueillement. Recueillement!* Reflection? Contemplation? Yes, but then considered as a "recognition" of the presence of "being", which is at work within me and confirms itself in me in faith and hope. Thus, I rediscover myself in my inner reality.

If philosophy wants to raise itself to the plane of
the second reflection, to push through to the authentic "being", if it does not want to break things up by
objective analysis, characterization and definition of
contents, then it will have to reflect on those experiences of "being" that contain the *pondus ontologicum*
(the highest weight of "being"), and in which one
rediscovers the "thinking about": fidelity, hope and
love.

Fidelity and Faith

"One of these days I promised C— that I would
visit him again in the hospital where he has been dying for weeks now. This is a promise that at the
moment I made it seemed to come from my inner-
most self. A promise carried on a wave of sympathy:
they have given him up, he knows it, and he knows
that I know. Since my visit, several days have passed.
The state of affairs that inspired my promise has not
changed, I cannot have any illusions on that score.
I ought to be able to say, indeed I dare say emphatically, that he still inspires me with the same sympathy. How could I explain a change in my interior
attitude, since nothing has happened that might have
altered it? Still, I must admit that the sympathy I
felt before is only a theoretical kind of sympathy
now. I am still of the opinion that he is miserable,
that he deserves sympathy, but a few days ago it
would not even have occurred to me to put it like
that. That was entirely superfluous. My whole being was just one irresistible urge of compassion
toward him, a helpless desire to help him, to show
him that I was with him, that his suffering was mine.

"I must admit that this spontaneous compassion
no longer exists. I am only able to imitate it by some

trick, but there is something in me that refuses to be
fooled by that. The most I can do is to say that
C— is miserable and lonely, and that I cannot leave
him alone; I have promised to visit him again; my
signature is on a check and he has that check in his
possession" (*Etre et avoir,* p. 46-47).

To what extent, we ask ourselves with Marcel,
have we kept a promise to someone who for weeks
has been at the point of death? Also, to what extent
have I been honest with myself? After all, did I not
pretend that I would remain faithful to a passing
sentiment? Indeed, if my "being" consists of mere
sentiments and desires of the moment, which are continually blown up by the wind and fluttering down
again, then I would not be able to give a satisfactory
answer to these questions. Of course, I can explain
that my feeling of sympathy at that moment has been
subjected to my later moods. But on the risk that I
may not fulfill my promise at all, or at least only par-
tially, my personality rises above this repeated rising
and falling of my sentiments and desires; I commit
myself in a *creative* process of fidelity for the future.

"*A fortiori* I have not been able to commit myself
to *feeling* the same way tomorrow as I did yesterday.
And still, when I try to discover what my promise
means insofar as it was an act—and here I leave out
of consideration what I was conscious of in that fleet-
ing moment—then I must admit that it contains a
binding precept, the audacity of which astonishes me
now" (p. 48).

In every promise I make abstraction from reality.
There is namely a territory between the "I" who bind
"myself" by a promise, and the current of causes and
effects over which I have no control. In this territory,
events take place that do not agree with my desires,

sentiments and expectations; events that are under
the influence of the moment. The faculty to make
abstraction of the actions that I performed in that
territory "lies in the very essence of my promise" (p.
48). By binding myself I rise above the *future* current of unforeseeable events. Hence I do not bind
myself to a continuous process of causes and effects,
but to a "being" that I cannot discern.

Now Marcel is confronted with the following alter-
native: at the moment when I make my promise, it
is either possible that I proceed from the unfounded
supposition that my sentiments are unchangeable, or
I agree beforehand that I will perform an act that
certainly will not reflect my interior attitude at the
moment I perform it. "And look, now there arises
again in my consciousness the memory of all the disappointments, all the feelings of resentment toward
myself and others, which are usually caused by hastily
made promises" (p. 50).

Is it just coincidences that are at play here, or
should we rather speak of a kind of presumption, of
which those hasty promises are the natural consequences? In order that we may maintain our inner
commitment, Marcel wonders if we should not learn
to close our eyes to that growing-process of causes
and effects that by force of habit we can no longer
distinguish:

"When I swear fidelity—whatever be the object
of my oath—am I not really obliging myself to deny
my most profound "being", to learn the trick of let-
ting myself continually be deceived by appearances
with which I have clothed myself? In short, is there
any commitment possible that is not treason? But
every treason is always reneged fidelity. Consequently, does there exist a fundamental fidelity, an orig-

inal commitment, which I break every time I swear an oath, and which is more or less significant for what I call in vague terms my soul?" (pp. 50-51)

I can understand this original commitment as the fidelity to myself. And here lurks the danger that my promise rests on the "supratemporal identity" of the "I", on my own will. It is a point of honor for myself to be faithful to the promise I made, not so much, or not at all, to the one who stands to benefit by my promise. In this way there is an egocentric accent on fidelity. Gabriel Marcel rejects this kind of fidelity: "How could I put this preoccupation of the soul with its own glory, after all, the most sterile, the most strained and cramped form of egoism, on a par with what I have always called fidelity?" (p. 53) Do we not find fidelity exactly in people who are not at all bent on shining in their own eyes, men and women who are ready to serve, mostly even those of humble origin? Russian literature of the last century, for example, is teeming with such "unobtrusive" types, but even today we meet them, even if we often think we don't!

Not in the tensile force of my own will, but in my "being", which interiorly binds that will, lies the principle-of-durability of my promise. And here it becomes clear that we must necessarily take "being" as our point of departure, our *being itself* as the commitment with regard to God. In fidelity there is an act of transcendency with an ontological reverse side, namely God's grip on me, by which *de profundis* (out of the depths) I make an appeal *ad summam altitudinem* (to the most high) (*Du refus à l'invocation*, p. 217). It is clear that only then God's grip has influence on me, when my appeal is based on the greatest possible humility. The acceptance of such a commitment is beyond my powers, but in the transcendental act of fidelity with regard to him in whom I have given my promise, he on his part is prepared to lend me all I need: "I can do all things in him who strengthens me", says St. Paul (Phil. 4, 13).

This absolute fidelity Marcel calls faith, and proceeding from this, our fidelity toward the other man, our fellowman, becomes possible. God himself, indeed, *le Toi absolu* (the Absolute Thou), present in faith, is the purest motive for our being committed to our neighbor. In that sense fidelity is a *fidélité créatrice* (a creative fidelity), genuine and authentic, because it always renews itself and thus shares in the infinite "being". An artist whose every work is a repetition of his previous one, is merely standing at his own assembly line, whereas a genius is always seeking new forms.

Fidelity toward our neighbor is based on fidelity toward God, the Absolute Thou, the center of all "being":

"Fidelity, especially there where it is most genuine, where it presents itself to us in its purest form, is accompanied by a disposition that in the highest thinkable degree is opposed to pride: patience and humility reflect themselves in the deepest recesses of its eyes. Patience and humility are the virtues that we have come to forget the very names of, and their nature is sinking to obscurity in the same measure as man's technical and impersonal equipment is being perfected, regardless of whether this is a logical or a dialectical equipment" (*Etre et avoir,* p. 56).

At the heart of fidelity as "experience" and fidelity as a "transcendental act" there is a relationship by which the "I" sees itself confronted with God as highest person. And God remains faithful to me, because in Him infidelity is impossible. This cannot be said of my fellowmen or of myself. According to Marcel, fidelity, seen ontologically, is perhaps the most important source of "being", because it is creative and permanent, i.e., eternal.

We just came to the conclusion that faith contains the *absolute fidelity*; it is an unconditional surrender of self. Marcel does not mean "believing *that* something is such or such", but "believing *in someone*". He is not in the first place concerned with dogmas, but with a person whom one adheres to and invokes.

"Faith, evidence of unseen things: I continually repeat to myself this enlightening definition, although it only becomes enlightening after the event. I also get an always clearer understanding of the role of the will in faith. It is a question of keeping oneself in a certain state, which on the human plane corresponds to grace. In this sense it is essentially a form of fidelity, the highest that exists" (*Etre et avoir,* p. 21).

As said before, God is the highest person, the Absolute Thou. As such He is God for me. May we consider God as an object, speak about Him and discuss Him as a "He"? That, after all, is what affirmative theology is also doing. May we, in other words, see God as a problem? Speaking about God as a "He" means that I am speaking about someone absent. And Marcel says: "The expression 'the problem of God' is undoubtedly in itself contradictory and even blasphemous" (p. 155). God as an absent "He" is an abstract, impersonal God. Nor are we allowed to pronounce judgment about God, who is above every judgment.

We must remark here, that theology — at least

sound theology—does not objectivize God, but exactly seeks Him as a person through His self-revelation
in Holy Scripture! Marcel's vision on theology is
merely polemic and therefore often one-sided and
without subtle distinctions. Indeed, I cannot prove
God. With the classical proofs of God's existence I
am powerless when I want to convince someone who
does not believe in God's existence. Because my belief in God is prior to proofs, nay even they presup-
pose belief and serve as an apologetic explanation
that is based on reason.

The arguments for the existence of God given by
St. Thomas Aquinas, however, are not meant to prove
God's existence, but to serve as a guide for the be-
liever, based on his own concrete experience of existence. "I believe" is a current expression; we pronounce it every day and we usually mean it in the
sense of "I suspect" or "in my opinion". Taken in
this sense, "I believe" seems much simpler and weaker
of meaning, even much less certain than the expression "I am convinced". If, however, we want to
penetrate the exact meaning of the term "believe"—
we already pointed this out—we have to direct our
attention not to believing in the sense of believing
that, but in the sense of believing *in.*

"Here we find the idea of 'credit', which can lead
us further. Establishing credit . . . that is, I think,
what faith as such really undertakes to do" (*Le mystère de l'être,* p. 78). Of course we must not let ourselves be blinded by the word "credit" as we use it in
business or banking. Because the bank expects a re-
turn of the money it lends us, within a certain time
and with interest. And if I fail in this, the bank has
the right to take the necessary steps. But with regard
to faith, "credit" is a different matter: *"When I be-*

lieve in, that means that I place myself at the disposal of, or rather, that I conclude a formal obligation not only with regard to *what I have,* but also to *what I am"* (p. 78).

Belief has an existential characteristic that in principle is missing in conviction, even if this conviction relates to this or that person's character, worth or merits. Conviction does not yet mean that there is a question of any binding obligation!

"If I believe in, I attach myself to, with a certain interior kind of gathering-together that this act carries with it. Seen thus, one might say that the strongest faith, or more exactly, the liveliest faith is that faith which most completely bundles together all the forces of your 'being' "* (p. 79).

Gabriel Marcel is of the opinion that this faith can always be translated into the language of conviction. We are thinking here of conversation with somebody, when I am *speaking* about my *faith.* And when I fully realize this faith I will come to treat it as a conviction. Therefore Marcel notices a distinction between faith as a commitment and faith as a conviction.

"Let us express ourselves once more, clearly: when I believe in God, and when one asks me questions about this faith or I question myself about it, I would of necessity have to declare, that I am convinced of the existence of God. But on the other hand, it seems that this translation ('believing' as 'being convinced'), which in reality is unavoidable, lets escape that which is original, and this is precisely its existential character" (p. 89).

Belief is the act of a free man who from his whole essence and "being" enters into an alliance with God. By faith I put myself at the *disponibilité* (disposal) of "being". But . . . "Instead of allowing the light of faith to shine through me, I usually darken it. In the measure in which I am not transparent, I do not believe. This is equally true of love or of *caritas*. Hence I cannot affirm that I believe without having to admit by a serious reflection on my insufficiency, that I do not believe; but this 'I do not believe' only becomes clear by the preceding 'I believe' " (*Du refus à l'invocation*, p. 223).

That "being" can neither be characterized, nor exhausted, and I cannot form myself any image of it. But Gabriel Marcel attempts to approach it positively in the *intuition aveuglée* (by blind intuition), by which I do not in the first place know, but *recognize* "being" (See "First and Second Reflection").

"This intuition does not reflect itself and cannot directly reflect itself. But by bending down over a whole world of thoughts it illuminates those thoughts and thus rises above them again. Speaking metaphysically, I do not see in what other way we could account for faith. I think that there is such an intuition at the base of every fidelity, but its reality can always be put in doubt. I can always say: 'Yes, I believed what I saw, but I was mistaken' " (*Etre et avoir*, p. 93).

Intuition aveuglée is belief, in which I recognize the mystery that surrounds me like a mist and keeps me surrounded.

Hope

"I am inclined to believe that hope is for the soul what breathing is for the living organism" (*Homo Viator*, p. 16).

Do we not feel a little—or perhaps very much—cheated in Albert Camus' *Le Mythe de Sisyphe*

(*Myth of Sisyphus*)? Do we really have to accept that Sisyphus, punished by the gods, is happy in his hopeless situation?

According to the Greek myth, Sisyphus had to roll a big block of marble by hand and foot up a hill. Every time he thought he had reached the top and let go of the stone, it rolled down the slope again and Sisyphus had to start again, time and time again, without any hope of success.

Albert Camus, however, thinks that it is possible that man can be happy in a hopeless situation. He has created the "absurd hero" for whom "the struggle for the top alone is enough". Sure of his failure and without resigning himself to it, Sisyphus has to go on with his task. In this way a logical and human experience such as hope comes to stand in an inhuman light.

"From the point of view of morality," Gabriel Marcel writes in *Les hommes contre l'humain,* "this conviction has much merit; it is honest, it is the conviction of a man who does not make himself any illusions and who wholeheartedly refuses to confuse what is with what he wishes" (p. 66).

However, Camus' conviction (he adds) is particularly naïve; it is that of a man who has not reached the "second reflection". Camus refuses to accept the idea that a world so brimful of misery could be the work of God. Marcel on the contrary writes: "Only in a world that *really can suffer damage* is there place for salvation" (*Etre et avoir,* p. 75).

In spite of that naïvete and of the exclusion of the metaphysical sphere, Camus' opinion is impressive for its fate-despising manly courage. It belongs perfectly in the sphere of Sartre's "absolute commit-

ment". It is moving by its sympathy with the name-
less misery in the world, but it repels by its hopeless-
ness. Must this really be the result of our efforts:
that we may no more hope for any result? If this
question is to be answered in the affirmative, there
can be no question of happiness:

"Hope is the property of disarmed people. It is
the weapon of the disarmed, or rather it is the oppo-
site of a weapon, and that is why it operates in a
mysterious way. . . . The skepticism of our time with
regard to hope consists in an essential inability to
understand that something can work effectively without being in any way a power in the usual sense of
the word" (p. 76).

But what is really the experience of existence that
we call "hope"? Gabriel Marcel will not attempt to
give its definition, the phenomenon is too complicated
and impalpable for that. He starts from the fundamental experience "I hope" and makes an appeal to
those he addresses and in whom he supposes this experience to be present. It is a question of approxi-
mation of the authentic experience of hope, which
only then gets its significance when the experience
"I hope", such as it presents itself to us in a first reflection, has been sifted out.

"We must not forget that the outcome of hope is
in the invisible world. We must not identify hope
with an emergency path, a detour for pedestrians,
which we use when the main road is blocked, and
which behind the obstruction brings us on that road
again" (p. 78).

There are two elements that we will always find
here: the wish, and a definite belief. But when I
say: "I hope that A—will come tomorrow", the wish

is present as a mere wish for daily use, i.e., not in the
existentialist meaning. Of course it may be extremely
important that A— will come, for example, in connection with my work, but "it is not really close to
my heart; the reasons for hoping are not rooted in the
soil of what I am" (*Homo Viator,* p. 46). The wish
is too superficial to touch my deepest inner being.

Moreover, one cannot imagine hope as being loose
from trial, whether this trial is individual or social;
we are thinking here of sickness, imprisonment, etc.
In both cases I hope for deliverance, liberation.
Hope is therefore included here in the situation in
which one finds oneself, it is the answer to trial, and
every trial of the kind mentioned above is a form of
imprisonment. And because we are always in situations that include temptations, we are essentially always "prisoners of" something.

"It is moreover typical for all the situations which
we have in mind here, that without exception they
include the impossibility for me not so much to move
about and act in a comparatively free way, but rather
*the impossibility to attain a certain fullness of life, a
fullness which may be that of experiencing, and even
that of thinking properly so called*" (p. 47).

Marcel quotes the example of the artist, who is
conscious of being in prison, when he is suffering
from prolonged unproductiveness. He is living in
"darkness", in a state of "estrangement".

Just as one can notice a big difference between
"I believe" and "I believe that", there is a difference
in tension between "I hope" and "I hope that". Marcel makes a distinction between hope and optimism.
The optimist takes it easy, he is the onlooker who,
as they say, knows how to look at things from a dis-

tance. In this way he can know and foresee that this
or that will turn out all right. Marcel points to say-
ings such as "Things always work out in the long
run", "The situation is no worse today", and "We
mustn't allow ourselves to become discouraged",
which are typical of the reasonings of optimists. In
opposition to those who have only a poor understanding of the course of events, the optimist counts
as an authority; his opinion hinges round his "ego".
He sees all things so extraordinarily clearly ("If your
eyes are as good as mine, it cannot escape you . . ."
(p. 53).

For the pessimist the above is equally valid, but
then in reverse. If, then, the subject of optimism
(and of pessimism) is a *moi* (myself) that puts itself
in the foreground, the subject of hope is a simple *je*
(I) without any pretension; we will come back to
this in the chapter entitled "I and Thou". The one
who hopes does not always know things better than
the other one, he does not foresee all things so accu-
rately and does not count on a satisfactory ending.

"The one who hopes sees himself as taken up in
a certain process, at least when he really hopes and
does not confine himself to platonic wishing. From
this point of view alone one can understand what is
the strictly proper, specific, suprarational quality of
hope, and perhaps even where it escapes all rela-
tions. Then hope appears to us not as a problem,
but as a mystery . . ." (p. 53).

One may—from the naturalistic point of view—
belittle hope, so that this experience becomes merely
some kind of a symptom of vitality in oppressive or
intolerable situations such as sickness, separation,
imprisonment, etc. But if exhaustion sets in, then hope
disappears ("Let no one have any illusion, hope is

nothing else but . . .") (p. 54). The authentic existential experience "I hope", however, refuses to cling to one thing or another; it does not weigh out the possibilities against one another, it rises above illusions and thus bans disappointments.

"We must therefore guard against the conviction that one can define hope by means of a psychological way of thinking; such thinking will always be based on hindsight, in order to explain something that in itself remains a mystery. If anyone wants to convince himself of this, it may suffice to remark that before the trial, we have no way of knowing how we will undergo it, and what forces we will appear to have at our disposal in order to resist it" (p. 55).

To hope also contains the temptation to despair. To despair means to lay one's head down, to capitulate, to resign oneself to a certain fate. Worse than that: "I resign" in face of the inevitable and renounce being myself, nay even to such an extent do I know myself to be condemned that I anticipate my own annihilation.

Suppose that I am incurably ill, that the doctors have given me up. What next? Well, I can accept my condition stoically. Even though I am no more than "a little heap of dirt in the festival hall" (to use an image of the author Willem Elsschot), I can still put against this my will to remain who I am; of my own free will I squarely face my fate.

If through my resignation my inner power increases, it will not eradiate, Marcel believes. The "ego" presents itself here in its highest expression of self-elevation: I alone carry responsibility for myself, I reject my fellowman.

This, therefore, is what the acceptance of destruction means. But what does hope do? It is not haughty, nor rebellious, and still it does not accept destruction. It is patient, it "takes its time" to overcome the trial: "But we glory also in our tribulations, knowing that tribulation worketh patience; and patience trial; and trial hope", writes St. Paul (Rom. 5, 3-4).

Hope requires from us a positive attitude. To hope is a dialogue between the "I" and the "thou"; there is a question of a "we"! That means, therefore, that the hoping man does not reject his fellowman, but rather tries to rise above himself and seeks to come in touch with society, of which as a man he is a part. He who hopes makes himself available: "The less someone is available, the less room he has for hope" (*Etre et avoir,* p. 78). Suicide is the most radical act of despair, of not-being-available. Marcel wonders whether the man who despairs of himself, has not already committed suicide in advance (p. 80)!

The metaphysics of hope cannot be other than Christian. It is therefore clear that hope, of which we just said now is a dialogue between the "I" and the "thou", appeals to the Absolute Thou that does not know infidelity. Hoping in God enables me to ward off the menace of despair. Because without Him I am nothing, and when I would declare that there is no longer any hope for me, this has the same meaning as: God has turned His back on me. And that is exactly what is so awful and absurd in despair.

What a sterile hero is this Sisyphus who was punished by the gods. How is it possible that he can be happy in his labor, which is eternally doomed to failure? Where does he get the courage always to go on with it? Where is he *human?*

Rising above time and this earthly life, our hope, like Moses on Mount Nebo, already sees the Promised Land before us. We cannot help quoting the canticle of canticles of hope; in the second part of the Epistle to the Romans (8, 19-27) St. Paul writes:

"For the eager longing of creation awaits the revelation of the sons of God. For creation was made subject to vanity—not by its own will but by reason of him who made it subject—in hope, because creation itself also will be delivered from its slavery to corruption into the freedom of the glory of the sons of God. For we know that all creation groans and travails in pain until now. And not only it, but we ourselves also who have the first-fruits of the Spirit—we ourselves groan within ourselves, waiting for the adoption as sons, the redemption of our body. For in hope were we saved. But hope that is seen is not hope. For how can a man hope for what he sees? But if we hope for what we do not see, we wait for it with patience. But in like manner the Spirit also helps our weakness. For we do not know what we should pray for as we ought, but the Spirit himself pleads for us with unutterable groanings. And he who searches the hearts knows what the Spirit desires, that he pleads for the saints according to God."

Have the existentialist philosophers, who take fear as their starting point, had their day? Marcel thinks so, if with some hesitation. In *L'homme problématique* he gives expression to this fear that they have shunted man on a dead track: "If they are able to renew themselves, then I am firmly convinced of it, they will have to do this by beginning to think about hope and joy" (p. 161).

5

Freedom Is
an Answer

"Come on, dear, it is high time you were in bed",
a mother says to her toddler; but he shows his dis-
pleasure in a loud voice. The child is so tired he can
hardly keep his eyes open, he obviously needs sleep,
but he still wants to stay up with the grown-up people.
That is why he uses his freedom to protest whiningly.
But his freedom is anything but adult, it is *liberté de
caprice* (uncontrolled and capricious). The child
does not yet really know what he wants.

"Where are you going this evening?" a father asks
his sixteen-year-old son.

"To a party with some friends", the boy answers vaguely.

"Which friends?"

The boy mentions a name that the father does not like.

"I don't want you to go there. Better see to it that your homework is perfectly in order."

But the boy says a bad word and a moment later he slams the front door behind him. His freedom has triumphed, *liberté de vainqueur*. He no longer lets his father lay down the rules for him, he wants to be autonomous.

A young man has been studying for some years and working a little here and there, but he has not yet seen his way to give direction to his life. Then he meets a girl with whom he falls in love. Now he has to make a decision: on the one hand, he is more or less leading an easygoing life, without any great responsibilities; on the other, he has the prospect of a regular job, with perhaps still more study, and marriage. The young man has *liberté de choix* (freedom to choose); his freedom is a freedom of choice.

Paralyzed by a disease, a woman is passing her days of life. She depends almost entirely on her husband, who looks after her with love and devotion, without carrying on an affair with another woman. His freedom is more than mere choice; it is *liberté d'engagement* (an inner commitment). In the situation in which this man finds himself, freedom coincides with love, which no longer seeks itself but the other one.

These are only a few examples by which to clarify the various forms of freedom such as they appear in

Gabriel Marcel's philosophy. Nor are these forms
necessarily bound up with definite periods of life,
although these periods are easily recognizable in
them. But when we look at the terrible game of politics, we see only too often how the freedom of the
toddler as well as that of the teen-ager is rearing its
ugly head there.

Strictly speaking it is impossible to give a description or a definition of freedom, because it is such a
personal thing and cannot be considered as a faculty
or some attribute. So there is no schematic freedom,
but only a thematic one. Freedom is a task, because
man has the freedom to make himself free. He is con-
tinuously *être en situation* (in some situation). The
milieu in which he was born, the nation to which he
belongs, the religious and political convictions that he
holds, his sphere of work, his talents and emotions,
etc., all these are factors that point to a continuous
being-in-a-situation.

We can also say that man participates in the situation in which he finds himself. And the freer he is, the
more he appears to be able to commit himself in his
situation; in other words, he *himself* decides the way
in which he commits himself. We repeat: man makes
himself free, he *becomes* free. His coming into this
life takes place beyond his will, and after his birth he
is still for a considerable time devoid of all knowledge
and completely dependent on his surroundings. But
the idea is that he will gradually develop and that his
personality will unfold itself. Contrary to God's freedom, however, which is unrestrictedly creative, man's
freedom should rather be called "giving meaning to"
than "creative of" things; it gives meaning to the situations in which he finds himself, within the limited
scope that has been given to him.

Let us with regard to the second example reflect for a while on the word autonomy. "I want to manage my own affairs: that is autonomy essentially put into words" (*Etre et avoir*, p. 163). Wherever *management* is possible, says Marcel, there is a question of autonomy. And autonomy lies in the sphere of our interests, which may be of a spiritual or a material nature. "To put it even more strongly: to a great extent I can consider my life as something that can be managed by someone else or by myself (in which 'myself' means 'not-the-other-one'). I can manage everything that, however little directly, can be equated with a faculty, with 'having' " (p. 163).

In a certain sense this is also applicable to talents; for example, literary and artistic ones. These, too, can be managed by the one who possesses them. But "for a genius who really escapes from himself, who crosses his boundaries in all directions, the idea of such a type of management is a complete contradiction in terms. A man *is* a genius, he *has* talent" (p. 163).

Autonomy belongs to the order of "having", freedom to the order of "being". Freedom is in essence non-autonomy. "The more I come into action integrally, the less I can say with justification that I am autonomous" (p. 164). Here we have in mind the freedom of the philosopher, the artist, and especially that of the saint.

How isolated and unconnected would experiences such as faith and hope become when we would say that Gabriel Marcel sees freedom in the sense of "I do what I want" or "I want to manage my own affairs." Involuntarily we see dictatorship, bureaucracy and anarchism, etc., looming up behind these seemingly not very alarming phrases. We must keep well

in mind that freedom is not the same thing as power.
The subject does not rule over his thinking and his
"being". If that were the case, then the subject would
be making himself his own prisoner in the solitude of
his pride; in other words, he would not be opening
himself to the other one. We are thinking, for example, of such a phenomenon as fanaticism, the natural
enemy of freedom, the little cuckoo-bird in the song-
bird's nest. Fanaticism, in the one who is afflicted
with it, does not only push freedom aside, but moreover aims at creating a No-Man's-Land around him
(Cf. *Le mystère de l'être,* p. 116).

Freedom in the sense of self-liberation, a humble
opening up of oneself to grace; this is how Marcel
understands it. Freedom is the cheerful answer to
someone else's call. I will only be really free when my
freedom can be understood in the sense of *partaking
in "being"*.

"Not a single answer from the outside will be able
to satisfy me, when it does not coincide with my own
answer, when it is not in the last resort *my answer"*
(p. 111). Freedom therefore coincides with the subject, with my conscious "I". "To say: I am, is to say:
I am I" (p. 115).

The attitude that I will assume with regard to my
life will be decisive for its evaluation. How will I stand
with regard to my marriage, my daily work, my talents, etc.? Shall I make use of my freedom to give
meaning to my life? Because ultimately that is the
point at issue.

"Freedom is essentially freedom of choice" (p.
116). But choice does not have the last word in the
matter of my freedom; it is rather to be considered as
a first preamble to my freedom with regard to the trial.
This trial, by virtue of its ambiguity, plainly requires

from me an *option fondamentale* (a fundamental free
choice) between hope and despair, between the possibility of liberation or imprisonment of my conscious
"I".

"Man can only be free or remain free in the measure
in which he remains connected with the transcendent,
and we may leave the form of this connection unspeci-
fied: it is only too clear that this form is not necessarily
covered by approved and fixed formulas of prayer"
(*Les hommes contre l'humain,* p. 19).

That Gabriel Marcel in the first place refers to that
freedom which proceeds from the inner person, admits, we think, of no misunderstanding. It is the interior surrender, the spontaneity of freedom, by which
also the prisoner can be a free man when he suffers
his punishment without bitterness and knows how to
give meaning to his imprisonment. Let us moreover
not forget this: "Even when we deny freedom, this is
an act where freedom, and freedom alone, makes itself felt" (*L'homme problématique,* p. 45).

Apart from the artist, who "creates" in a special
sense, every human being is capable of (limited)
"creation" — let us just call to mind the *fidélité
créatrice* (creative fidelity).

"And as a creator, however humble the level may
be at which this creating takes place, every human
being can recognize his freedom. But then one should
not lose sight of the fact that this 'creating', taken in
that general sense, always implies a standing-open to
the other man" (*Les hommes contre l'humain,* p. 20).

6

I and Thou

"*L'enfer c'est les autres*" (Hell is the other person),
says Jean Paul Sartre (*No Exit*). Gabriel Marcel
speaks of "a certainty which seems to have been lost
in our time: the honor of being man" (*Les hommes
contre l'humain*). We are not going to probe into the
question: which of the two is right? That would be, in
our opinion, sterile and, moreover, simplistic. Sartre's
pronouncement is hard and carries the temptation to
agree with it—at least that is how it is with us.

In the political sphere, in our family life, in our
daily work—whether we are manager or subordinate
—we experience all the time that infidelity and treason
are the order of the day, and it looks indeed as if we
simply cannot help being hell to the other man. In

this sense we may perhaps understand *"L'enfer c'est les autres"* as a comforting pronouncement, especially in moments when we are filled with self-pity. But it does not satisfy us in the long run; the consolation is too meager for that; we do not feel any less uncomfortable for it; we are seeking warmth near a stove in which there is a dying fire.

Against this certainty of Sartre's, Gabriel Marcel puts his brand of certainty: the honor of being man. That is another consoling pronouncement! And we cannot escape, but we have to agree with this one, too. Sartre's "hell" shuts off, Marcel's "honor" opens . . . what a number of possibilities, all of a sudden! Possibilities of fidelity, faith, hope and especially love. Not that this certainty must necessarily inspire us to raise our voices in *Alle Menschen werden Brüder* (All men become brothers), but think of the possibilities that it gives us! Not as already realized, but for realization.

Let us leave capricious and often satanic politics out of consideration, but who has on account of them (war, exile, etc.), or in his family life, or in his daily work, never once experienced that there can be such sentiments as fidelity, faith, hope and love? Who has never during a concert, a conversation, the contemplation of a work of art or the reading of a book experienced the honor of being a man?

Some sort of a meeting must be possible in which we discover in our fellowman something other than our hell. And the more we stress the personality of the "I" in our being, and the special nature of our existence, the more it becomes clear that confronting the "I" there is someone else, a "thou", for whom I must open myself, if I want to discover a little who I really am myself. For my *entre en situation* (being in a situation), friendship is an indispensable good.

What matters is "that each one of us must recognize or discover himself in all the others, without losing in the process any part of what is his inner being. And the philosophical reflection is going entirely in the same direction" (*L'homme problématique,* p. 64).

If we may speak of the "discovery" of the subject, then the name of honor of "discoverer" is due to the French philosopher René Descartes (1596-1650). His *Cogito ergo sum* (I think, therefore I am) has given the first impulse to subjectivism. Descartes in particular has put full weight on consciousness, such as no philosopher before him had done.

Since that discovery, how much fighting has taken place on the frontier of human thinking! And we are still nowhere near the end of the fight. In the Idealism of Immanuel Kant's (1724-1804) Critical Philosophy, the process of subjectivizing was more and more extended, and Friedrich Hegel (1770-1831)—with his *absolute Geist* (absolute spirit)—made by his Absolute Idealism a completely rounded-off whole of human thinking. Everything fitted perfectly, but no place had been made for the struggling and suffering fellow-man; in the enormous palace of thought there were only rooms available for absolute spirits. The subject cut itself off from its co-subjects.

How differently Gabriel Marcel is thinking! Because he starts from the concrete experience of existence rather than from universal reason. Against the completely-being-in-oneself (solipsism) of the Idealists he puts the being-in-society of concrete persons. He does not confront us with *the* thinking, but with *"I" and "thou" who "think"*. Marcel sees Descartes' *Cogito* as a becoming aware of one's own existence; but then in the empirical sense: I am the *conscience de moi* (object of my perception).

"While I am thinking, I take some distance from myself (my "I"); I attain the perspective of "the other one", and consequently I emerge as existing" (*Etre et avoir,* p. 99). I experience myself as distinguished from others. Idealism has identified this empirical consciousness with *conscience de soi* (transcendental consciousness). We need not explain further that Gabriel Marcel cannot agree with this. We know that man is an *être incarné,* bound to matter and time. My "being" is an *être en situation* (being in a situation) and I experience it as a *limited* "being", whence there arises a desire for compensation for this limitation. As *être incarné* I am only a particle of the entire "being", I am living among fellow beings: the others. Being with those others is a dimension of my incarnate "being", it is a *co-esse* (being-together).

Being man means participating in one's fellowman. Seen in this way, friendship is a compensation for my limitation. Here we can speak of a subject-subject relationship. Confronting the "I" there stands a "thou" as a person, not a "he" as a thing or an object.

Yes, man is a *free* being, he can shut himself off from the other man and look upon him and treat him as object. But what then does Marcel mean by the meeting between "I" and "thou"? The answer is: an invitation. Two human beings open themselves up for one another, *invocation, appèl* (appeal), to one another in a free, inner movement of love, by which they break through their narrow individuality and thus become themselves. A new subject originates, a "we".

The meeting is not an approach from the outside, it is *métaproblématique* (problem solving). With this word Marcel seeks as it were to impress upon us that objectivization is no longer possible. To be with others is in the concrete experience to be *recognized* as a mystery. It is obvious that the meeting thus obtains a metaphysical aspect. In opposition to a *communication objective* there is a *communication ontologique*. The conscious "I" enters into the concrete experience, and from there it tries to push through to the mystery of "being". It is in my relationship with the other one that the process of my becoming a person takes place. I do not want to comprehend the other one methodically, but rather to re-enter into myself (*recueillement*) in the concrete experience of being with the other. Together we are involved (*engagement*) in "being", and the "I" opens itself (*disponibilité*) for the presence of the "thou" in its entirety, just as the "thou" does this for the "I".

Conscience de soi is not yet a *conscience de moi*, it is an imperfect consciousness. My becoming conscious of my existence in the world points the way to the existence of the other man and my relation with him. The other man is the instrument by which I can measure my victories or my defeats. I want him to pay attention to me; in other words, the "I" wants to see his own existence confirmed by the other man. Automatically the thought comes up now that the nature of such a relationship is one of subject-object.

The simplest example from daily life illustrates this better than the best philosophical definition, Gabriel Marcel believes. In *Homo Viator* he gives us the example of a child who has picked flowers for his mother. "Look, *I* picked those!" The child really means: "It was *me*, and *nobody else*." He offers his mother more than just flowers, he offers *himself*, because *he* has picked them. *C'est moi* (it is myself) the French say pointedly, in opposition to the unpretentious *je* (I).

"It is very instructive to devote a careful description to the act which really constitutes what I call 'I', by

which I point out myself to the other to harvest his
praise—or in other cases his blame—but in any case
to draw his attention. In all those cases it can be said
in the ontological sense of the word that I 'generate'
myself, that means that I place myself in the foreground" (pp. 23-24).

The egoist is another example, although much less
innocent than the child. The egoist shows us the sorry
picture of the man who, in his becoming a person, has
not fully developed. With regard to himself as well as
with regard to the other one, he is sneaking behind the
prison bars of his subject-object cell. Locked up in
his narrow, well-circumscribed little world he is always occupied with himself and carefully marks the
boundaries of *his* domain. The other one is for him
a menace, or the opportunity to give more prestige to
his own existence. This egocentrically directed man
uses the other man as a sound-amplifier that is at his
disposal. He regards him in whatever manner is more
convenient. In this way it becomes possible that the
other man is seen as a mere phantom, a substitute of
the other man, to whom the egoist tunes in his words
and actions.

The egoist lives in an *espace mental* (a closed mental space) with his "I" as the center. He has assumed
a *crispation* (convulsive attitude) with regard to his
own "being", which he treats as "having". To illus-
trate this, we point to Marcel's analysis of the "pose"
in *Homo Viator*:

"The one who strikes a pose and who outwardly
appears to be only full of the thoughts of others, is in
reality only full of himself. For he is only interested
in the other one insofar as he can be used to form a
favorable image of him, which he can then again appropriate to himself. The other one merely reflects the

image in which he (the viewer) takes delight" (pp. 26-27).

"Fundamentally one is always striking 'poses' for oneself. One may speak of 'posing for the gallery', but the gallery, the public, that is again oneself. Even more pointedly one could say that the other one is merely the provisional and in a sense accidental medium by which I succeed in forming a certain image, a certain idol of myself. One really ought to go into detail to find out by what stylizing process everyone fashions this image. Both in failure and success this process finds favorable conditions for development" (p. 28).

The above shows us clearly how far the "I" is still remote from any thought of a subject-subject relationship with the other one. The other one is merely a threat to the boundaries that the "I" has drawn up around its little world. And a threat not even as a person, but as a "something", an object that must be resisted. We may call the fear of what others may think of me the basic motive for every "border" conflict.

How can the "I" free itself from the enclosure of its egocentricity and achieve a *je-tu* (I-thou) relationship in the "meeting"? This word has in Gabriel Marcel's philosophy a loaded meaning. He really wants to indicate by it an "inter-human" contact that has nothing to do with chance or with some conventional relationship. Meeting, therefore, is not in the sense of two political leaders or two football teams who "meet" one another, nor in the sense of an acquaintance whom one has "met".

In the meeting such as Marcel envisages here, the "I" breaks open its *topographie égocentrique* (egocentrical topography) and through this opening it becomes accessible to the appeal that can be made to it by the other one with whom it has come into contact. In this way it becomes possible that the "I" begins to entertain feelings of sympathy, nay even of friendship toward that other person, even though it is not impossible that such a meeting is of a passing nature and may leave sadness and uncertainty behind in the "I". But such an experience is salutary, Marcel says, because the egocentric "I" is jolted by it in its self-sufficiency; it is completely "swept off its feet" by it, as we say. "To meet somebody is not merely to cross his path; it is at the least to be for a moment close to him, with him; it is a co-presence" (*Du refus à l'invocation,* p. 20).

The special character of the subject-subject relationship is that it makes the other one present to the "I" in a *mysterious way;* the other one is co-present as a "thou". The possibility has been created to come to a dialogue, to develop oneself from *moi* to *je* (from "myself" to "I"). The "I" is no longer isolated, because there is an answer, coming from the other one. The answer will not decide whether we can indeed speak of a meeting. The answer always occurs in a conversation; but are the countless opinion polls and interviews to which we are subjected really conversations? Has not the answer in such cases merely information value, while man is merely used or misused as an object for study or for sensation? The value of the person is being diminished in this way. It is indeed not by what I "am" but by what I "have" that I am pigeonholed.

Also, in the company of our friends or colleagues, where the social lie is often a social necessity (which one lets out just as one has to let the dog out), the human person does not come close to himself, let alone close to others. The "Everyman's-Land" of the social meeting is at the same time a "No-Man's-Land", where no real dialogue is held, but where one has "conversation". The other one as "thou" is absent. In the real dialogue the stress is on the being-together of "I" and "thou", and the answer means a revelation of the "thou" to the "I". The one has nothing to hide from the other.

"When I treat the other one as *thou*, then I treat him, I grasp him, as freedom, because he *is* also freedom and not merely nature. Stronger even, in a certain sense I am helping him to be freedom, I cooperate toward his freedom, words that may sound extremely paradoxical and contradictory, but which are time and time again recognized as true by love" (*Etre et avoir*, p. 101). If the dialogue must be fruitful, then it will at a given moment have to turn into a monologue. Question and answer will fall away, because both subjects themselves *are* question and answer. The being-present of the one partner in the dialogue appeals to the "being" of the other one, and that other one responds by making himself present, he makes himself available. Goethe says somewhere: *"Ich kenn den Menschen nicht, weil ich noch nie mit ihn geschwiegen habe"* (I don't know the man because I have never kept silence with him).

The meeting is not just an interaction but a *reciprocal* intercourse of "I" and "thou" who get to know one another as persons. Because meeting has a metaphysical aspect for Marcel, we must not forget that the "I-thou" relationship must not only be present when the one subject converses or keeps silence with the other, in a way visible for outsiders, but also when the "I" gets a letter from the "thou", by which they are all the same present to one another. The "I" shares in the well and woe of the "thou", and appears to himself as it were by surprise as "another man". It experiences its "being-person" in a "we". This does not obtain when the letter contains a mere notification, and therefore points to a business relationship between two people (Cf. *Journal métaphysique*, p. 171). In the first case there is *"une valeur proprement onto-logique de l'émotion"* (the emotion has value that is ontological, properly so-called). The emotion reveals to us the being-with-the-other! The man who is sitting next to me in the bus is not in the strict sense riding *with* me in the bus. He is a perfect stranger to me, and therefore not "present" to me. If I get into conversation with him, the little word "with" begins to take on some meaning.

I am neither for myself nor for the other man a completely transparent reality, and for this reason: in my most inner being I am involved in the greatest mystery of all: the personal, transcendental God, *le Toi absolu*. By ignoring this mystery, man has lost the realization of his own "being" and that of the others as a mystery. We have become a problem for one another.

Marcel makes a passionate plea for the restitution of the value of the person in our time, in which the devaluation of the human personality is on the increase, and in which being businesslike seems to be the greatest virtue, and technical science the supreme good.

The meeting is for man both a gift and a task. Fidelity, faith, hope and love are fused together in the relationship between the "I" and the Supreme Thou, to whom the poet Friedrich Hölderlin once addressed

himself in his first *Christushymne* (Hymn to Christ)
in these words:

Redeemer, you who, though never believed,
are present here now, you who take the form
of my friend, Immortal One. . . .

7

The Mystery

Repeatedly in the course of this introduction the word "mystery" has been used without our probing more deeply into its meaning. The mystery determines the light-intensity of the whole of Marcel's thinking. Whether we are reflecting on "my body", or on fidelity, faith, hope, the "meeting", everywhere we find the twilight of the mystery. There is no day and no night in Marcel's philosophy, there is a continuous twilight, in which the believing man has the presentiment of the coming of a beautiful, eternal day.

Let us say this first: the mystery is not the same thing as a problem. There is a great distinction between the two. It is in the regions of objective thinking that the problem is in its element. In principle, it is something that can be solved and broken up into small parts. "The problem is something we come across, something that blocks our way. It is entirely before me" (*Etre et avoir,* p. 95).

The scientist occupies a privileged position with regard to the problem. With his intellect he aims at repairing the breach that every problem carries with it, in order that it may not slow down a certain development. "Progress is only a matter of *problématique*" (problematic knowledge) (p. 96).

The mystery, however, is not something that can be solved or split up into small parts; it is not an atom:

"The mystery is something in which I feel myself involved, and the essence of which is therefore that it is not entirely before me. It looks as if in this field the distinction between what is *in me* and what is *before me* loses its meaning" (p. 95).

The mystery is therefore immediately connected with "being", and with regard to this there is only one question possible that I can ask myself: what is "being"? From this there follows a second question: who am I who question myself about "being"? The first question implies that I myself am connected with this mysterious "being"; the second question implies that the mystery as such cannot be objectivized, but asks for recognition in a concrete existential experience.

There is a great temptation to make mystery into a problem, by which I really reduce it to the level of a problem. Because "being" is not susceptible to analysis, it is in its entirety impenetrable. And therefore it is fruitless to sit down to unravel the mystery.

Marcel puts a typical problem before us: evil. He compares it to an accident that has occurred to a machine—the world—or rather, "I pretend that evil is an accident" (p. 95). It goes without saying that Marcel does not follow up this comparison, because exactly by considering evil as an accident, I reduce it to a problem. "In this way I do not only act as if I had not been effected myself by that sickness or that weakness, but as if I were standing outside the world which—at least ideally—I am trying to repair in its integrity" (p. 95). Indeed, evil touches myself and it makes me suffer. How then can I look upon it from a distance and judge it without taking sides? Evil is, as Marcel expresses it, *métaproblématique* (of a metaphysical nature), it is lost in the mystery.

There exists also an absolute contrast between secret and mystery. Let us proceed here from the distinction between "having" and "being", which is really bound up closely with the distinction between problem and mystery.

What is the characteristic mark of "having"? That it has always, directly or indirectly, something to do with the world of things, it indicates a certain externality with regard to myself. "What I have is added to me" (p. 145). It is of course possible that there originates a tie, even a strong tie, between myself and the thing I possess, by which this thing becomes, as it were, an intimate part of myself. But in spite of this it cannot be freed from its externality. Now we can distinguish two forms of "having": having in the sense of "possessing", and having in the sense of "including", or having by implication. When I say I have a bicycle, or I have my opinions about this or that, there is purely a question of possessing.

"Including is what I am doing when I say: 'My body has this quality' " (p. 150). In other words, that quality seems to me to be something interior, something that is rooted in the interior of my body. And an interesting example of this is the "having" of a secret. "This secret is only secret by the fact that I keep it, but also and at the same time because I could give it up" (p. 150). The essence of the mystery, however, is that I have no hold over it, I cannot dispose of it.

Attached to the mystery—and to everything where there is a having in the strong sense of the word—is the fear of discovery or treason, the worry that I could lose my possession. "Because to say 'I have' can only have meaning in the context of opposition to someone else felt as 'the other' " (p. 151).

Characteristic for "having" is that it admits of being exposed. I can show the drawings of a friend or my own to someone else. Also his ideas are "exposable". I can even say that I am someone else, insofar as I expose my thoughts to myself.

The kind of "having" that covers the area of analysis and *problématique* and that is connected with things and objects can never become a "being" in which I share by virtue of my subjectivity. "Being" surpasses all "having"; it is present in me and forms my inner being.

All the same, Marcel points out that "having" can transform itself into "being", wherever there is a question of pure creative work. This is applicable for instance to the laboratory of the scientist, the piano of the musician, the ranch of the farmer. Because in such cases the matter is continually renewing itself to become some personal creation. This is also important with regard to immaterial possessions such as my thoughts, my opinions. But we must not forget: only there where we can speak of creative activity, not of rigid activity.

Let us still reflect for a moment on the distinction, already hinted at in the above lines, between problem, secret and mystery.

A problem is in principle capable of solution; it can be analyzed and understood; it involves technology. With a problem I have data at my disposal that I work out.

A secret can be discovered or betrayed; I can also voluntarily give it up.

A mystery cannot be solved; it is a problem that does not admit of delimitation; it is, as Marcel says, *métaproblématique*. It must be recognized. I cannot dispose of it as of a problem and a secret, which lie within the boundaries of "having". It involves my "being". If man wants to confront the mystery, on which he depends and outside of which he is nothing, then he will have to open himself through those means that have been given to him for this purpose, means that Gabriel Marcel calls "central activities": religion, art and metaphysics.

Epilogue

What do people think of Marcel's philosophy?

"Vacation-reading", says one man, who considers Jean Paul Sartre's *L'être et le Néant* (*Being and Nothingness*) alone as a philosophy that is worth reading.

"A little gloomy", says another, who does not take such a gloomy view of life, of his *être au monde*.

Two reactions to Gabriel Marcel's philosophy.

We will leave the first for what it is: conceited, if not blasé.

We will stop for a moment at the second opinion. A little gloomy? Marcel does give this impression here and there in his philosophy. His book *Les hommes contre l'humain* especially does sometimes seem to reflect a rather gloomy outlook on life.

Moreover, Marcel's philosophy cannot be exonerated from one-sidedness. He throws a particularly unfavorable light on science and objective thought. In his book *Gabriel Marcel et Karl Jaspers* (chapter

2, pp. 157-158), Paul Ricoeur remarks that one does not find in Marcel any extensive treatment of typically sociological questions, such as functions, the institution-concept, the meaning of history. Ricoeur ascribes this among other things to the fact that Marcel is rather pessimistic with regard to the spirit of modern times, which he criticizes on three points: (1) the technological age—man's desire for "having" (possessions); (2) the spirit of collectivity—mass-mentality, impersonality; (3) the abstraction — the *Cogito: la non-insertion en acte* (a philosophy that does not enter into actual life).

What Marcel's philosophy lacks is a positive reflection on the meaning of technical science. The machine is, after all, an extension of my body. From the incarnation idea, therefore, one cannot only deduct the meaning of the body, but also the meaning of a technical instrument. Therefore one cannot just pass over the history of the technical evolution. In other words, to wish for a state of the sciences of some centuries ago is as silly as to wish for a different body.

If one philosophizes about man, one must understand him as he is given to history, in this case, as "modern man". It would be desirable for existentialist philosophy always to have the ability to incorporate the spirit within the "context of time". Furthermore, Marcel does not give us any positive reflection on the meaning of law, the institutions in our human society, etc. As a matter of fact, all forms of law rest on a foundation of an *abstraction* that is altogether indispensable. That is why we speak of *the* human being. Marcel's mistake is that he confuses this abstraction, the technical sciences, democracy and the impersonal way of thinking of the scientist, and puts them all on one level. A transcendental philosophy such as Gabriel Marcel's has exactly the task to maintain the distinction between these various stages of human existence, and to attach to each its positive value at its own level.

So far, briefly, a few reservations with regard to Marcel's philosophy at the hand of Paul Ricoeur.

But when Dr. Josef Vital Kopp, in his excellent book on Pierre Teilhard de Chardin remarks that Teilhard "can do nothing with the apocalyptic lamentations of the existentialists", we feel that we have the duty toward the positive, Christian "existentialist" Gabriel Marcel, to enter a protest against the expression "apocalyptic lamentations". We are thinking here of the oppressive problem of evil in this world, and Dr. Kopp might perhaps lead his readers astray with this disparaging remark; as if existentialism had somehow lost its right of existence thanks to Teilhard's vision. Probably he did not mean it like that, but one may well conclude this from his words. We agree that Marcel, too, occasionally laments apocalyptically, but surely not always without reason.

Teilhard de Chardin's vision is grand, and for many —also for us—indispensable to holding on to Church and faith in these exciting, crucial and extremely difficult times. Marcel is somewhat hesitant in accepting the idea of a cooperation between religion and science as Teilhard sees it. Teilhard, however, does not know very well what to do with evil in this world; he more or less reduces it to a trifle. Marcel emphatically points out this evil, to which also the technical sciences, in spite of their many blessings, contribute in no small degree. He warns us against it. Here the correcting power of the existentialist way of thinking comes to the fore. In whatever way humanity may develop for the better in the future, we cannot—not even scientifically—neglect the evil of today, which in all its monstrous forms and excesses, and with all the misery it causes, is not only part of our reality, but also largely determines this reality.

We still come back for a moment to the one-sidedness of Marcel's philosophy, and ask ourselves the question: which philosophy can really claim to be free of one-sidedness, unless it is sitting on the fence?

Has not Marcel's one-sidedness been caused mainly by an honest sympathy at the sight of the multiple sufferings of others? "Marcel does not condemn the practice of science, technology, politics, commerce, etc., at all. He realizes very well that they are absolutely necessary for us in this world. The danger, however, is that man becomes so engrossed in the desire for 'having' and becomes so external, that he has no longer anything internal, or more exactly, that he can no longer enter into himself, be himself" (Dr. B. Delfgaauw, in his Introduction to the Dutch edition of *Etre et avoir*).

For us, therefore, Gabriel Marcel is a unique thinker as far as his concepts of the meeting, fidelity, hope and the mystery are concerned. We do not consider him as a perfect man, although we would like to do so on account of his philosophy. But perhaps a personal meeting with him might well be disappointing. And would we then find ourselves sufficiently humane to accept him as a man, with all his changing moods? Would we still want to continue to see in him a unique thinker, in spite of the fact that we would probably slink off disappointed? We have not met Marcel personally, but we dare say that he would be the first to recognize that there is only one perfect man, the Socrates of the Gospels: Jesus of Nazareth, the only one who completely is what he thinks and does.

Prof. Dr. H. Robbers, S.J., thinks that Marcel's philosophy is not far from mysticism. His philosophy is an ontology of hope and sanctity (*Bijdragen,* Neth., S.J. iv, 1941).

"Gabriel Marcel is always assured of a circle of readers," Etienne Gilson believes. "In his work man is directly in conversation with man: it will always have readers, because he [Marcel] will never cease to make new friends" (*Existentialisme chrétien,* p. 2).

We want to conclude by saying that Gabriel Marcel, with his philosophy of the meeting, fidelity, hope and the mystery, has made a really positive contribution to the indispensable, impressive, although never completed edifice of human thought. His neo-Socratism is indisputably permeated with Christian revelation.

"It is obvious that an ontology that is thus directed, stands open in the direction of a revelation. It cannot indeed demand a revelation, or suppose it, or integrate it, and it cannot even—strictly speaking—comprehend it, but to a certain extent it can prepare for its acceptance" (*Etre et avoir,* p. 113).

He further points to the "essential similarity of Christianity and human nature" (*Du refus à l'invocation,* p. 109). The light of the Christian mystery is gradually beginning to shine through the frosted-glass window of the ontological mystery. The incarnation of Christ is revealing itself in the incarnation of man in the world. "Hence the more deeply one penetrates into human nature, the more one puts oneself at the center of the Christian truths" (p. 109).

In this way, then, Gabriel Marcel's philosophy climbs up by way of the "thou" to the Thou that is

God, the Supreme Thou, the Absolute Being within human experience, to Him in whom we rediscover *engagement*, *fidélité* and *amour* in their most perfect form.

Bibliography

Philosophical Works by Gabriel Marcel

Journal métaphysique (1927)

La métaphysique de Royce (1945).

Etre et avoir (1935).

Du refus à l'invocation (1940).

Homo Viator (1945).

Positions et approches concrètes du mystère ontologique (1949).

Le mystère le l'être I et II (1951).

Les hommes contre l'humain (1951).

Le déclin de la sagesse (1954).

L'homme problématique (1955).

Philosophical Works by Gabriel Marcel in English Translation

Metaphysical Journal, trans. Bernard Wall (Chicago: Regnery, 1952).

Royce's Metaphysics, trans. Virginia and Gordon Ringer (Chicago: Regnery, 1956).

Being and Having, trans. Katherine Farrer (Boston: Beacon Press, 1951).

Homo Viator, trans. Emma Crauford (Chicago: Regnery, 1951).

Philosophy of Existence, trans. Manya Harari (New York: Philosophical Library, 1949). Contains translation of *Positions et approches concrètes du mystère ontologique.*

The Mystery of Being, 2 vols. (Chicago: Regnery, 1951). Vol. I: *Reflection and Mystery,* trans. G. S. Fraser. Vol. II: *Faith and Reality,* trans. René Hague.

Man Against Mass Society, trans. G. S. Fraser (Chicago: Regnery, 1952).

The Decline of Wisdom, trans. Mayna Harari (London: Havrill Press, 1954).

DEUS BOOKS
Popular Paulist Paperbacks

Specially designed to fill the widespread current need for popular treatments of religious and social topics underlying the contemporary scene. Each is timely, stimulating, solidly informative.

THE ADVENT OF SALVATION by Jean Danielou, S.J. Since we say it is possible for those outside the Church to be saved, why do we insist that everyone ought to be a Catholic? 95c

UNLESS SOME MAN SHOW ME by Rev. Alexander Jones. A book to meet the need for Catholic biblical literature, solid in substance yet attractive in form. A surprisingly cheerful book on Old Testament interpretation. 95c

WHAT IS THE CHURCH? by Donal Flanagan. For the interested layman and for the priest who wishes to brush up his theology and to obtain fairly easily a bird's eye view of the fruit of some of the recent trends in ecclesiology. 95c

COMMUNISM TODAY: BELIEF AND PRACTICE by Victor Ferkiss, Ph.D. Presents to the average reader, in non-technical language, a picture of Communism, without bias or distortion. 95c

ECUMENICAL COUNCILS OF THE CATHOLIC CHURCH by Hubert Jedin. A brief and proportioned account for the general reader of the most important previous Councils and the issues they decided. (Available in U. S. only.) 95c

THINK AND PRAY by Joseph McSorley, C.S.P. A series of object lessons for those who are learning the art of communing with God. The central doctrines of Catholicism are covered. For group and private meditation. 95c

HANDBOOK FOR NEW CATHOLICS by Aloysius J. Burggraff, C.S.P. Contains all the "little things" new Catholics need to know which cannot be covered in basic instructions. Ideal gift for converts. 95c

WHAT IS A SAINT? by Jacques Douillet. Like "What Is Faith?" this paperback needs no introduction to the many thousands who cherish the original clothbound edition. 95c

WHAT IS FAITH? by Eugene Joly. A paperback reprint of a clothbound volume that has been very, very popular with readers. 95c

THE SPLENDOUR OF THE CHURCH by Henri de Lubac, S.J. A meditative attempt on the part of the author to work himself, and his readers, into the heart of the mystery of the Church. $1.25

SHAPING THE CHRISTIAN MESSAGE, ed. Gerard S. Sloyan. This book gives special attention to the problems of the "new catechetical movement" of the last fifty years. It incorporates the answers that a number of educators have given to the most fundamental question of our times: how are the young to be formed, and not merely instructed, in accordance with the living message of Jesus Christ? 95c

THE LIFE OF FAITH by Romano Guardini. One of the foremost European theologians of our times analyzes what faith means as an experience in ourselves and others. He examines the relationship of faith to action, love, hope and knowledge, and the Church's part in fostering and preserving the life of faith in each of its members. 75c

JOSEPH THE SILENT by Michel Gasnier, O.P. A historical reconstruction of Joseph's life and a study of his spirituality. In no sense is this a fictional or imaginative work; it follows closely the Gospel narrative and takes into account the teachings of the Church. 95c

FREEDOM OF CHOICE IN EDUCATION by Virgil C. Blum, S.J. A challenging study setting forth the reasons why the State and Federal Government, to be effectively engaged in education, ought to distribute benefits to those who attend private schools. For parents, educators, lawyers and members of the clergy. 95c

MYSTICS OF OUR TIMES by Hilda Graef. This collection of biographies of ten mystics of the past one hundred years shows that a life of spirituality and mysticism can be lived by individuals engaged in the ordinary pursuits of business and living. Each combined contemplation with active lives. Each profoundly transformed the circle in which he or she lived and each is a source of inspiration to modern readers. An original approach to an ever-inspiring subject: the personal life of man with God.   95c

A SELECTION OF CONTEMPORARY RELIGIOUS POETRY, ed. Samuel Hazo. In his choice of poems for this selection, Samuel Hazo shows how mid-century poets—primarily in America—have faced the facts of life within their own age before they refused, accepted or transcended them. The English Departments of high schools and colleges will welcome this book.   95c

WITNESSES TO GOD by Leonard Johnston. The Bible has become so well worn in our civilization there is a need for something to help you see it fresh. This is what this book helps the reader to do. It is written with liveliness and wit, yet with a full weight of expert scholarship behind it.   95c

THE FASCINATING FEMALE by Dorothy Dohen. Every woman, married and single, will recognize the problems discussed by the author and be interested in her suggestions for a happy family life. This book has been written for the American Catholic woman primarily. In it Dorothy Dohen blends psychological, sociological and religious perspective with unusual success. Every woman will want to have a copy.   95c

LIFE AND LOVE: THE COMMANDMENTS FOR TEENAGERS by Daniel Lowery, C.SS.R. This book is meant especially for high school students. The emphasis is that the duties and responsibilities of Catholic living should not be looked upon as just so many "do's" and "don't's". The challenge of the faith is to see how much God has loved us, and to respond to God's love. A splendid text for high school classes in religion.   95c

CHRISTIAN FAMILY FINANCE by William J. Whalen. Drawing upon a wealth of experience, common sense, and detailed professional knowledge, the author discusses home-owning, furniture, credit and installment buying, insurance, food, clothing, recreation, health, taxes, investments, charity, social security and retirement. A book for husbands and wives and all engaged in family counseling.   95c

COUNCIL SPEECHES OF VATICAN II, ed. Hans Küng, Yves Congar, O.P., Daniel O'Hanlon, S.J. "To praise this collection of 51 Council speeches would be like praising Shakespeare or the Bible. . . . It will undoubtedly become a Catholic classic." **Catholic World** (A Catholic Book Club Selection)   **$1.25**

A BIBLIOGRAPHY FOR CHRISTIAN FORMATION IN THE FAMILY by Mother Marie Aimee Carey, O.S.U. This bibliography is intended for parents in order to aid them in fostering a genuinely Christian family life and in fulfilling their responsibilities toward the religious and moral training of their children. It also serves as an excellent guide for religious teachers, directors of Family Life groups in their role of counseling parents of children from pre-school years through elementary school.   95c

LIVE IN HOPE by Walter J. Sullivan, C.S.P. Stimulating encounters with St. Paul, Cervantes, Sophocles and Newman: these one-page reflections offer adventure among the masterpieces. Essays on **Macbeth, Hamlet, Winter's Tale, Troilus and Cressida, As You Like It,** and **Richard II** afford enticing meditations for a Shakespearean year. All essays are calculated to engender hope.

RETREAT FOR BEGINNERS by Ronald Knox. A series of conferences that Msgr. Knox gave to boys in retreat at school. This book reveals the author's keen insight and wisdom as he speaks directly and forcefully to young men. As has been the case for every one of Msgr. Knox's published works, whether they are addressed to a particular or general audience, this book will appeal to the general reader just as much as it will appeal to young men.   95c

LITURGY IN FOCUS by Gerard S. Sloyan. How the liturgy is something quite distinct from rubrics, how the Eucharist is at the center of the liturgy, how the sacraments are not just passing events in the life of every Christian, but are daily operative in their lives. No matter what point or problem of the liturgy Fr. Sloyan discusses, each chapter implements the idea that the liturgy is meant to mold and fashion the lives of every Christian, that it is not merely the commemoration of what once existed, but that it is living and real.   **95c**

A KEY TO THE PARABLES by Wilfrid J. Harrington, O.P. Here are all the parables of the New Testament places in their original setting—the ministry of Jesus. Father Harrington demonstrates conclusively how most of us are surely unaware that the parables, as they stand in the gospels, may not have quite the same meaning they had when first spoken by our Lord. In other words, if we cannot to some extent at least establish the original sense of a parable, it is obvious that we are going to miss something of its true meaning.   **95c**

ECUMENICAL THEOLOGY TODAY by Gregory Baum, O.S.A. The ecumenical movement is constantly expanding in the Christian world and it is the purpose of this book to explain and analyze the significant events and theological developments associated with this movement. This book consists of 30 articles, each is distinguished by its creative approach to theological questions. This book is divided into five parts: Problems of the Council, The Catholic Church, Ecumenical Developments, Ecumenical Dialogue, Christians and Jews. **95c**

A MAN NAMED JOHN F. KENNEDY, ed. Charles J. Stewart and Bruce Kendall. Twenty-five sermons—selected from 850 from 50 states and Washington, D. C.— by the American clergy (Protestant, Catholic and Jew). An eloquent as well as an historical record of the representative words and reactions of the American clergy. (Requests of sermons went to nearly 2,000 clergymen.)
$1.25

A GUIDE TO PACEM IN TERRIS FOR STUDENTS by Peter Riga. Weaving his book with a strong thread of charity, Fr. Riga both instructs and admonishes, touching upon the plethora of problems that plague today's world: unemployment, racism, colonialism, human rights, economic rights, underdeveloped countries, etc. This book does not have to be restricted to Catholic high schools; its message is broader.   **95c**

THE LITURGY CONSTITUTION with study-club questions and complete text of the Constitution and Motu Proprio of Paul VI. A chapter-by-chapter analysis of the Constitution on the Sacred Liturgy for the many people who may find it difficult at times to perceive the full import of the Constitution. Six authors of special competence, who had been in touch with the liturgical movement for years, divided the Constitution between them, and each took the sections in which he was most competent. Through their combined efforts they provide in this book the liturgical and theological context which the Constitution presupposes and in which its significance is perceived more fully.   **95c**

FOUR CONTEMPORARY RELIGIOUS PLAYS, ed. Robert J. Allen. "The Shadow of the Valley" by Jan Hartman, an original 3-part mystery cycle in prose and verse, dramatizing the crisis of faith in the modern world; "Once There Was A Postman" by Robert Crean, a 1-act father-son drama of superb sentiment; "The Broken Pitcher" by Leo Brady, a 1-act drama of conflicting loyalties set in a Red Chinese prison which holds three American Air Force men; "Without The Angels" by Robert Crean, a wacky 1-act comedy, satirizing "pat" religious art. Preface by Pulitzer Prize winning historian-novelist, Paul Horgan. Eight pages of photos from the TV productions of these plays on the CBS and NBC Networks. All plays adapted for stage production. **95c**

UNDERSTANDING PARENTHOOD by Charles and Audrey Riker. An informal and practical handbook about children and their development.   **95c**

SOCIAL ASPECTS OF THE CHRISTIAN FAITH CONTAINED IN MATER ET MAGISTRA AND PACEM IN TERRIS by Mother Maria Carl Haipt, O.S.U. Adopted for implementation of the religious syllabus of the New York Archdiocese. Provides background and material and a discussion of concepts basic to an understanding of the Church's social teaching. Aims to open the way to a more enlightened Christian action in our times.   **75c**

THE ENEMIES OF LOVE by Dom Aelred Watkin. In this meditative and instructive study of the subject of love the author shows that human love (if rightly understood) is divine love translated into the terms of human experience. He examines the assaults which selfishness makes upon that love and indicates where and how they may be overcome.   **95c**

JESUS: A DIALOGUE WITH THE SAVIOUR by a Monk of the Eastern Church. Sometimes our pretentious and complicated apostolates of today create the false impression that the man of today cannot hear Christ without all kinds of explanations, rearrangements and especially without endless preparation. In this work, however, the author is able to make every man hear Christ from the very first word. In his forty short meditations he recaptures the words and scenes of the Gospel and succeeds in helping us rediscover and appreciate more fully that very springing forth of the Word of God. **95c**

THE CATHOLIC QUEST FOR CHRISTIAN UNITY by Gregory Baum, O.S.A. A balanced study of the contemporary movement for Christian unity in the Church and other Christian communities, this work studies the new attitude this movement has produced in the Catholic Church. It will open new vistas for the individual reader who desires to widen his work for Christian unity and will give him a new insight into the Church's ecumenical task.   **95c**